S E R I E S

A life-changing encounter
with God's Word from the books of the

MINOR
PROPHETS 1

HOSEA, JOEL, AMOS,
OBADIAH, JONAH & MICAH

A NavPress resource published in alliance
with Tyndale House Publishers, Inc.

NAVPRESS◑

NavPress is the publishing ministry of The Navigators, an international Christian organization and leader in personal spiritual development. NavPress is committed to helping people grow spiritually and enjoy lives of meaning and hope through personal and group resources that are biblically rooted, culturally relevant, and highly practical.

For more information, visit www.NavPress.com.

CONTENTS

HOW TO USE THIS GUIDE

Along with all the volumes in the LifeChange series of Bible studies, this guide to the Minor Prophets shares common goals:

1. To provide you with a firm foundation of understanding, plus a thirst to return to the books of the Minor Prophets throughout your life.

2. To give you study patterns and skills that help you explore every part of the Bible.

3. To offer you historical background, word definitions, and explanation notes to aid your study.

4. To help you grasp as a whole the message of the Minor Prophets.

5. To teach you how to let God's Word transform you into Christ's image.

As you begin

This guide includes twelve lessons that will take you chapter by chapter through the first six books of the Minor Prophets. Each lesson is designed to take from one to two hours of preparation to complete on your own. To benefit most from this time, here's a good way to begin your work on each lesson:

1. Pray for God's help to keep you mentally alert and spiritually sensitive.

2. Read attentively the entire passage mentioned in the lesson's title. (You may want to read the passage from two or more Bible versions—perhaps at least once from a more literal translation such as the New International Version, English Standard Version, New American Standard Bible, or New King James Version and then once more in a paraphrase such as *The Message* or the New Living Translation.) Do your reading in an environment that's as free as possible from distractions. Allow your mind and heart to meditate on the words you encounter—words that are God's personal gift to you and to all His people.

After reading the passage, you're ready to dive into the numbered questions in this guide that make up the main portion of each lesson. Each of

5

these questions is followed by blank space for writing your answers. (This act of writing your answers helps clarify your thinking and stimulates your mental engagement with the passage as well as your later recall.) Use extra paper or a notebook if the space for recording your answers seems too cramped. Continue through the questions in numbered order. If any question seems too difficult or unclear, just skip it and go on to the next.

Each of these questions will typically direct you back to the Minor Prophets to look again at a certain portion of the assigned passage for that lesson. (At this point, be sure to use a more literal Bible translation rather than a paraphrase.)

As you look closer at a passage, it's helpful to approach it in this progression:

Observe. What does the passage actually *say*? Ask God to help you see it clearly. Notice everything that's there.

Interpret. What does the passage *mean*? Ask God to help you understand. And remember that any passage's meaning is fundamentally determined by its context. So stay alert to all you'll see about the setting and background of the Minor Prophets, and keep thinking of these books as a whole while you proceed through them chapter by chapter. You'll be progressively building up your insights and familiarity with what they're all about.

Apply. Keep asking yourself, *How does this truth affect my life?* (Pray for God's help as you examine yourself in light of that truth and in light of His purpose for each passage.)

Try to consciously follow all three of these steps as you shape your written answer to each question in the lesson.

The extras

In addition to the regular numbered questions you see in this guide, each lesson also offers several "optional" questions or suggestions that appear in the margins. All of these will appear under one of three headings:

Optional Application. These are suggested options for application. Consider these with prayerful sensitivity to the Lord's guidance.

For Thought and Discussion. Many of these questions address various ethical issues and other biblical principles that lead to a wide range of implications. They tend to be particularly suited for group discussion.

For Further Study. These often include cross-references to other parts of the Bible that shed light on a topic in the lesson, plus questions that delve deeper into the passage.

(For additional help for more effective Bible study, refer to the "Study Aids" section starting on page 135.)

Changing your life

Don't let your study become an exercise in knowledge alone. Treat the passage as *God's* Word and stay in dialogue with Him as you study. Pray, "Lord, what do You want me to notice here?" "Father, why is this true?" "Lord, how does my life measure up to this?"

Let biblical truth sink into your inner convictions so you'll be increasingly able to act on this truth as a natural way of living.

Consider memorizing certain verses and passages you come across in your study, ones that particularly challenge or encourage you. To help with that, write down the words on a card to keep with you and set aside a few minutes each day to think about the passage. Recite it to yourself repeatedly, always thinking about its meaning. Return to it as often as you can for a brief review. You'll soon find the words coming to mind spontaneously, and they'll begin to affect your motives and actions.

For group study

Exploring Scripture together in a group is especially valuable for the encouragement, support, and accountability it provides as you seek to apply God's Word to your life. Together you can listen jointly for God's guidance, pray for each other, help one another resist temptation, and share the spiritual principles you're learning to put into practice. Together you affirm that growing in faith, hope, and love is important and that you need each other in the process.

A group of four to ten people allows for the closest understanding of each other and the richest discussions in Bible study, but you can adapt this guide for other-sized groups. It will suit a wide range of group types, such as home Bible studies, growth groups, youth groups, and church classes. Both new and mature Christians will benefit from the guide, regardless of their previous experience in Bible study.

Aim for a positive atmosphere of acceptance, honesty, and openness. In your first meeting, explore candidly everyone's expectations and goals for your time together.

A typical schedule for group study is to take one lesson per week, but feel free to split lessons if you want to discuss them more thoroughly. Or omit some questions in a lesson if your preparation or discussion time is limited. (Group members can always study further on their own at a later time.)

When you come together, you probably won't have time to discuss all the questions in the lesson, so it's helpful for the leader to choose ahead of time the ones to be covered thoroughly. This is one of the main responsibilities a group leader typically assumes.

Each lesson in this guide ends with a section called "For the group." It gives advice for that particular lesson on how to focus the discussion, how to apply the lesson to daily life, and so on. Reading each lesson's "For the group" section ahead of time can help the leader be more effective in guiding the group.

7

You'll get the greatest benefit from your time together if each group member also prepares ahead of time by writing out his or her answers to each question in the lesson. The private reflection and prayer this preparation can stimulate will be especially important in helping everyone discern how God wants you to apply each lesson to your daily life.

What to do in your time together

There are many ways to structure the group meeting, and you'll want to vary your routine occasionally to help keep things fresh.

Here are some of the elements you can consider including as you come together for each lesson:

Pray together. It's good to pause for prayer as you begin your time together as well as to incorporate a later more extensive time of prayer for each other, after you've had time to share personal needs and prayer requests (write these down in a notebook). When you begin with prayer, it's worthwhile and honoring to God to ask especially for His Holy Spirit's guidance of your time together.

Worship. Some groups like to sing together and worship God with prayers of praise.

Review. Discuss what difference the previous week's lesson has made in your lives, and recall the major emphasis you discovered in the passage for that week.

Read the passage aloud. Once you're ready to focus attention together on the assigned Scripture passage in this week's lesson, read it aloud. (One person could do this, or the reading could be shared.)

Open up for questions. Allow time for group members to mention anything in the passage they may have particular questions about.

Summarize the passage. Have one or two people offer a summary of what the passage says.

Discuss. This will be the heart of your time together and will likely take the biggest portion of your time. Focus on the questions you see as the most important and most helpful. Allow and encourage everyone to be part of the discussion for each question. Take written notes as the discussion proceeds. Ask follow-up questions to sharpen your attention and deepen your understanding of what you discuss. Give special attention to the questions in the margins under the heading "For Thought and Discussion." Remember that sometimes these can be especially good for discussion, but be prepared for widely differing answers and opinions. As you hear each other, keep in mind each other's various backgrounds, personalities, and ways of thinking. You can practice godly discernment without ungodly judgment in your discussion.

Encourage further personal study. You can find more opportunities for exploring this lesson's themes and issues under the heading in the margins called "For Further Study" throughout the lesson. You can also pursue some of these together during your group time.

Focus on application. Look especially at the "Optional Application" listed in the margins throughout the lesson. Keep encouraging one another in the continual work of adjusting your lives to the truths God gives in Scripture.

Summarize your discoveries. Read aloud through the passage one last time together, using the opportunity to solidify your understanding and appreciation of it and clarify how the Lord is speaking to you through it.

Look ahead. Glance together at the headings and questions in the next lesson to see what's coming next.

Give thanks to God. It's good to end your time together by pausing to express gratitude to God for His Word and the work of His Spirit in your minds and hearts during your time together.

Get to know each other better. In early sessions together, spend time establishing trust, common ground, and a sense of each other's background and what each person hopes to gain from the study. This may help you later with honest discussion about how the Bible applies to each of you. Understanding each other better will make it easier to share about personal applications.

Keep these worthy guidelines in mind throughout your time together:

Let us consider how we may spur one another on toward love and good deeds.

(HEBREWS 10:24)

Carry each other's burdens, and in this way you will fulfill the law of Christ.

(GALATIANS 6:2)

Accept one another, then, just as Christ accepted you, in order to bring praise to God.

(ROMANS 15:7)

THE MINOR PROPHETS

Major Messages from Across the Centuries

The final twelve books in our Old Testament have together been grouped and perceived as a collective unit for millennia. "In Ecclesiasticus (an Apocryphal book written c. 190 B.C.), Jesus ben Sira spoke of 'the twelve prophets' as a unit parallel to Isaiah, Jeremiah, and Ezekiel. He thus indicated that these 12 prophecies were at that time thought of as a unit and were probably already written together on one scroll, as is the case in later times. Josephus also was aware of this grouping. Augustine called them the "Minor Prophets," referring to the small size of these books by comparison with the major prophetic books and not at all suggesting that they were of minor importance."[1]

"All of the so-called twelve minor prophets of the Old Testament have their distinctive features, so there is no sense of monotony as we move from one to the next."[2]

"Their authors lived and labored as prophets at different periods, ranging from the ninth century B.C. to the fifth; so that in these prophetic books we have not only the earliest and latest of the prophetic testimonies concerning the future history of Israel and of the kingdom of God, but the progressive developments of this testimony. When taken, therefore, in connection with the writings of the greater prophets, they comprehend all the essentials of that prophetic word through which the Lord equipped His people for the light and power of His Spirit."[3]

Timeline

The dating for some of the books in the Minor Prophets is rather uncertain, but the following list is a suggested chronology.

Obadiah (in the reign of Joram, king of Judah) — between 889 and 884 BC
Joel (in the reign of Joash of Judah) — between 875 and 848
Jonah (in the reign of Jeroboam II of Israel) — between 824 and 783

Amos (in the reigns of Jeroboam II of Israel and Uzziah of Judah) — between 810 and 783

Hosea (in the reigns of Jeroboam II of Israel and Uzziah, Jotham, Ahaz, and Hezekiah of Judah) — between 790 and 725

Micah (in the reigns of Jotham, Ahaz, and Hezekiah of Judah) — between 758 and 710

Nahum (in the reign of Hezekiah of Judah) — between 710 and 699

Habakkuk (in the reign of Manasseh or Josiah of Judah) — between 650 and 628

Zephaniah (in the reign of Josiah of Judah) — between 628 and 623

Haggai (in the reign of Darius of Persia) — in 520

Zechariah (in the reign of Darius of Persia) — between 520 and 480

Malachi (in the reign of Artaxerxes of Persia) — between 433 and 424[4]

1. *NIV Study Bible*, introduction to "The Book of the Twelve, or the Minor Prophets" (Grand Rapids, MI: Zondervan, 1985).
2. Leland Ryken and Philip Graham Ryken, eds., introduction to Habakkuk, "The Book at a Glance," *The Literary Study Bible* (Wheaton, IL: Crossway, 2007).
3. C. F. Keil and F. Delitzsch, *Commentary on the Old Testament: The Minor Prophets*, vol. 10 (Edinburgh, UK: Clark, 1871; Peabody, MA: Hendrickson, 1996), 2.
4. Adapted from Keil and Delitzsch, 3.

HOSEA 1–3

God's Love for a Sinful People

Hosea's ministry "embraced the critical years of religious decline and decay in the northern kingdom, from about 750 B.C. until a few years before the fall of Samaria in 722 B.C. Hosea's preaching focused on Israel's breach of her covenantal relationship with God, mixing the pure worship of the Lord with the idolatry of the surrounding peoples (religious syncretism), and on the impending judgment. However, Hosea's proclamation of the nature of God's love sounds a more positive note in the book."[1]

"The vividness of the poetry and figurative language is a striking feature of the book [of Hosea], as God's people (for example) are pictured as an oven or a stubborn heifer or wild grapes. Even though the failed and restored marriage of Hosea and Gomer is present only in

Optional Application: After Jesus' resurrection, when He was explaining Old Testament passages to His disciples, He "opened their minds so they could understand the Scriptures" (Luke 24:45). Ask God to do that kind of work in *your* mind as you study the book of Hosea so you're released and free to learn everything here He wants you to learn and so you can become as bold, worshipful, and faithful as those early disciples of Jesus. Express this desire to Him in prayer.

For Thought and Discussion: How familiar to you is the book of Hosea? What have been your previous impressions of this book?

the first three chapters, the controlling metaphor of covenant Israel as an unfaithful wife exerts an implied presence throughout the book."[2]

"Despite the punishment that God promised to bring upon them, there is a strong attitude of hope that is evident throughout the book. Just as Hosea bought back his unfaithful wife, Israel will be redeemed by God in the last days."[3]

1. For getting the most from all these books of the Minor Prophets, one of the best guidelines is found in 2 Timothy 3:16-17, words Paul wrote with the Old Testament first in view. He said that *all* Scripture is of great benefit to (a) teach us, (b) rebuke us, (c) correct us, and (d) train us in righteousness. Paul added that these Scriptures completely equip the person of God "for every good work." As you think seriously about those guidelines, in which of these areas do you especially want to experience the usefulness of the books of Hosea, Joel, Amos, Obadiah, Jonah, and Micah? Express your desire in a written prayer to God.

_____

_____

_____

_____

2. Think also about these words of Paul to Timothy: "Do your best to present yourself to God as one approved, a worker who does not need to be ashamed and who correctly handles the word of truth" (2 Timothy 2:15). As you study God's Word of Truth in the Minor Prophets, the Lord calls you to be a "worker." It takes *work* — concentration and perseverance — to fully appropriate God's blessings for us in this book. Express here your commitment

before God to work diligently in this study of the Minor Prophets.

I need to know more about these prophets

Hosea (1:1). This name "comes from the same verb as 'Joshua' and 'Jesus,' meaning 'to save or deliver' (Hebrew *yasha*)." [4]

---

3. What do you know already about the kings mentioned in Hosea 1:1?

they reigned in the 7th century B.C.

4. In Hosea 1:2-3, what does the Lord command His prophet to do and why? How does Hosea respond?

marry an adulterous woman because the land is guilty of adultery who has children of unfaithfulness

---

The Lord said to him, "Go, marry a promiscuous woman" (1:2). The command states literally, "Go take to yourself a wife of fornications." [5] "The thing everyone remembers about the book of Hosea is that God tells the prophet to marry a prostitute. This is, indeed, a shocking but true premise. Throughout the entire Bible, marital and sexual imagery is regularly used as a

For Further Study: For more background on the kings mentioned in Hosea 1:1, see 2 Kings 15:1-7 and 2 Chronicles 26:6-23 (for Uzziah, also known as Azariah); 2 Kings 15:32-38 and 2 Chronicles 27:1-9 (for Jotham); 2 Kings 16 and 2 Chronicles 28 (for Ahaz); 2 Kings 18–20 and 2 Chronicles 29–32 (for Hezekiah); and 2 Kings 14:23-29 (for Jeroboam, son of Joash).

For Thought and Discussion: What's the "shock value" of the Lord's asking one of His prophets to marry a woman who proved herself to be an adulterer? What would appear to be God's point in this?

metaphor for the relationship between God and those who believe in him. Believers who are true to God are a chaste bride; those who are apostate are an adulterous prostitute. The book of Hosea turns that metaphor into a living reality, though the reality, of course, is intended as a metaphor for the faithless covenant people of Israel (the northern kingdom)."[6] Scholars differ on whether Gomer was already guilty of sexual promiscuity before she married Hosea or whether it was only after their marriage that she became adulterous.

Children of whoredom (1:2, ESV). Or "children of harlotry" (NASB, NKJV). The phrase is literally "children of fornications."[7] "The implication of this literal rendition of the command is that the prophet married an unchaste woman and, at the same time, adopted the children who were already hers because of her sexual promiscuity."[8] These children would then be joined in the family (after Gomer's marriage to Hosea) by the siblings whose birth is mentioned in verses 3, 6, and 8. It would be these three youngest children who are addressed in 2:1, where "brothers" and "sisters" would refer to Gomer's earlier children. However, many scholars hold that only one set of children is in view.

Jezreel (1:4,5). "Literally, 'God sows' or 'plants.' This is the name of a beautiful and fertile valley between the mountain ranges of Samaria and Galilee (the site of Gideon's victory over the Midianites, Judges 6:33), and of a town at the valley's southern end, where Jehu came to power through violence (1 Kings 21:1; 2 Kings 9–10). This valley became the place of judgment in 733 B.C. (2 Kings 15:29). This punishment through military defeat suggests the theme of covenant breaking since it reflects the curses recorded in Leviticus 26:17; Deuteronomy 28:25,49-57. Yet Jezreel is also a sign of blessing and fertility in Hosea 2:22."[9]

curses
before
Mose

5. What does the Lord promise to do in Hosea 1:4-5?

_Put an end to the kingdom
of Israel, He will break Israel's
bow in the Valley of Jezreel_

Israel's bow (1:5). "Israel's military strength, symbolized by the bow, was broken by the Assyrian army under Tiglath-Pileser III, who conquered the northern territories of Israel."[10]

---

6. In 1:6-7, what promises does the Lord make concerning His people?

"I will show love to the house of Judah and I will save them — not by bow, sword or battle, or by horses and horsemen, but by the Lord their God

---

Lo-Ruhamah (1:6). Or "No Mercy" (ESV). "The child's name signifies the imminent withdrawal of the compassion God had shown to Israel in spite of her covenant unfaithfulness."[11]

---

7. In 1:8-9, what does the Lord ask Hosea to do and why? What significance do you see in this?

_(Gomer)
She is to call her son
Lo-Ammi, God is punishing
them for being unfaithful
and turning away from him_

Lo-Ammi (1:9). Or "Not My People" (ESV). "The naming represents a break in the covenant relationship between the Lord and Israel (see Exodus 6:7; Jeremiah 7:23), which later, however, would be restored (see Hosea 1:10; 2:1,23). The warnings become more severe in moving from the first to the third child."[12]

8. What are the promises made to God's people in 1:10-11?

the Israelites will be like sand on the seashore (uncountable) and will be called "Sons of the Living God

9. In Hosea 2:1-5, what messages and what warnings does Hosea receive from God for the people, and for what reasons?

they are to rebuke the unfaithful and if they do not change and come back to God he will punish them by taking away their food and resources

My lovers (2:5). Referring to "the pagan idols that Israel worshiped. Israel trusted in these idols for prosperity."[13] See also 4:10-19; 5:4; 9:1,10. God's hatred of religious syncretism (the mixing of true and false religion) is seen throughout the book.

10. What does the Lord promise concerning His people in 2:6-8, and what does this communicate about His complaint against them?

He will block Israels path so that they will return

18

Which they used for Baal (2:8). "Hosea's major concern was the worship of Baal—an apostasy that he understood to be the reason for Israel's dilemma. Baal was the weather-god worshiped in Syria-Palestine, who had control over agriculture and fertility, rainfall and productivity. Since ancient Israel was always an agricultural society, Baal worship was of unrivaled importance. . . . One major aspect of Baalism touches on this prophet's message: the religion's appeal to human sexuality (see Isaiah 57:3-10). . . . Hosea understands the strength of Baalism's appeal to the sex drive by way of ritual prostitution."[14]

11. Summarize what the Lord promises to do in 2:9-13.

   God will take away all the resources of the people, stop all celebrations and festibals to the moons. He will punish them by destroying their vines and figtrees which came from her lovers.

12. What is most significant in the Lord's promise to His people in each of the following passages, and what does this communicate about His heart for them?

   a. 2:14-15

   He will lead them into the desert where he will speak to them, then he will give them back their vineyards and make the Valley of Achor a door of hope and they will be happy.

   b. 2:16-20

   the people will come back to the Lord forgetting the names of Baals. God will make a covenant with them and all beasts of the fields and birds of the air, He will betroth them forever in rightousness and knowledge of the Lord

19

Optional Application: Review the Lord's loving words of commitment to His people in Hosea 2:19-20. To what degree can you receive and embrace these words as coming from the Lord to you? What do they mean for you? What do they offer to you?

For Further Study: How does the message you've seen so far in the book of Hosea link most closely with God's words spoken through the prophet Jeremiah in Jeremiah 2?

c. 2:21-23

God will make the earth respond to grain, new wine and oil and they will respond to Jezreel (God plants)

Valley of Achor (2:15). "Literally 'Valley of Trouble,' this area was located near Jericho and was the site of the stoning of Achan (Joshua 7:24-26). Though associated with sin and death, this valley was to be transformed into a 'door of hope.'"[15]

I will betroth you to me forever; I will betroth you in righteousness and justice, in love and compassion (2:19). "Here the qualities of righteousness, justice, love, mercy, and faithfulness are a sort of bride-price that guarantees the permanence of the relationship."[16] "These attributes come only from the Lord (Exodus 34:6-7) and are precisely what Israel desperately lacks. This is in harmony with the divine initiative represented by the many 'I wills' in Hosea."[17]

You will acknowledge the Lord (2:20). Notice how this theme recurs in 4:1; 5:4; 6:3,6; and 13:4. *Acknowledge* translates a Hebrew word that "seems to be a technical term for covenant intimacy, loyalty, and obedience."[18]

---

13. In Hosea 3:1-3, what does the Lord ask His prophet to do and why? How does he respond?

Go and live with his unfaithful wife and love her as the Lord loves the Israelites. Hosea bought his wife for 15 shekels.

Fifteen shekels of silver and about a homer and a lethek of barley (3:2). "The payment,

20

roughly half in silver and half in produce, amounted to about thirty shekels and approximated the price of a slave in Exodus 21:32."[19]

14. What does the Lord promise concerning the people of Israel in 3:4?

Live without king or prince without sacrifice or sacred stone, without ephod or idal.

Without king or prince, without sacrifice or sacred stones, without ephod or household gods (3:4). "Today the people of Israel have no king, they do not practice idolatry, and they no longer observe the Levitical institution of sacrifices. The prophet had no basis on which to prognosticate these things in the day in which he lived. It is a remarkable prediction."[20]

Last days (3:5). "The Hebrew for this phrase occurs 13 times in the Old Testament, sometimes simply meaning the future, but most of the time, as no doubt here, referring to the Messianic age ('afterward,' Joel 2:28; see Acts 2:17; Hebrews 1:2)."[21]

---

15. What does the Lord promise concerning His people in 3:5, and what is the significance of this?

They will return and seek God and David their king and come trembling to the Lord and to his blessing in the last days forgiven as a lord

16. How would you summarize the way Hosea's family life serves as a prophetic symbol in chapters 1–3?

It was symbolic of the way Israel had become but God still considered Israel worth saving

21

_____

_____

_____

17. In Hosea 1–3, what would you select as the key verse or passage—one that best captures or reflects the dynamics of what these chapters are all about?

verse 2 — he was to take an adulterous wife + her children because it symbolized the way Israel had become

√2-3

18. What do these chapters in Hosea communicate most to you about the heart and character of God?

God is a father, teaches and punishes as required to instill character and belief in the one God

word picture for life

19. From what you see in these chapters, what does God especially want us to understand about the relationship He desires with His people?

He wants us to be faithful and follow his teachings and rules for living

20. List any lingering questions you have about Hosea 1–3.

_____

_____

_____

_____

For the group

In your first meeting, it may be helpful to turn to the front of this book and review together the section "How to Use This Guide."

Consider focusing your discussion for lesson 1 especially on some of the following issues, themes, and concepts recognized as major overall themes in Hosea. Which of these are dealt with in some way in chapters 1–3, and how are they further developed there?

- Human sinfulness *God forgives — go and sin no more*
- Our repentance
- God's justice and judgment
- God's love
- God's uniqueness and holiness
- Apostasy and restoration

In particular, questions 16–20 in lesson 1 are among those that may stimulate your best and most helpful discussion.

Remember to look also at the questions in the margins under the heading "For Thought and Discussion."

1. *New Geneva Study Bible*, introduction to Hosea, "Date and Occasion" (Nashville: Thomas Nelson, 1995).
2. Leland Ryken and Philip Graham Ryken, eds., introduction to Hosea, "Format and Distinguishing Features," *The Literary Study Bible* (Wheaton, IL: Crossway, 2007).
3. Warren Baker, ed., *The Complete Word Study Old Testament* (Chattanooga, TN: AMG Publishers, 1994), introduction to Hosea.
4. *ESV Study Bible* (Wheaton, IL: Crossway, 2008), at Hosea 1:1.
5. Thomas Edward McComiskey, "Hosea," *The Minor Prophets* (Grand Rapids, MI: Baker, 2009), 12.
6. Ryken and Ryken, "The Book at a Glance."
7. McComiskey, 12.
8. McComiskey, 12.
9. *New Geneva*, at Hosea 1:4.
10. *New Geneva*, at Hosea 1:5.
11. *New Geneva*, at Hosea 1:6.
12. *NIV Study Bible*, (Grand Rapids, MI: Zondervan, 1985) at Hosea 1:9.
13. Baker, at Hosea 2:5-13.
14. *ESV*, introduction to Hosea, "Purpose, Occasion, and Background."

15. *New Geneva*, at Hosea 2:15.
16. *New Geneva*, at Hosea 2:19.
17. *ESV*, at Hosea 2:19.
18. *New Geneva*, introduction to Hosea, "Characteristics and Themes."
19. *New Geneva*, at Hosea 3:2.
20. McComiskey, 54.
21. *NIV Study Bible*, at Hosea 3:5.

HOSEA 4–7

God's Case Against Israel

1. In Jeremiah 23:29, God says that His Word is "like fire" and "like a hammer." He can use the Scriptures to burn away unclean thoughts and desires in our hearts. He can also use Scripture, with hammer-like hardness, to crush and crumble our spiritual hardness. As you continue in your study of the Minor Prophets, how do you most want to see the fire-and-hammer power of God's Word at work in your life? Express this longing in a written prayer to God.

_____

_____

_____

_____

2. As Hosea 4 begins, God is like a courtroom prosecutor, stating His case against His people Israel. Summarize His case as you see it unfolding here in chapter 4.

no faithfulness, no love, no acknowledgment of God in the land only evil living, stealing, adultery

25

For Thought and Discussion: What are the inner hindrances that so often keep people from seeking or returning to the Lord?

3. What kinds of punishment does God sentence His people to in chapter 4?

destroy your mother, reject your priests, ignore your children, punish your priests and you

---

The land dries up (4:3). "God's judgment on man's sin affects all living things in man's world (see, for example, Isaiah 24:3-6; Jeremiah 4:23-28)."[1]

4. In light of the message for Israel (the northern kingdom) in chapter 4, what meaning and significance do you see in the warning to Judah (the southern kingdom) in verse 15?

do not be like the rest of Israel, stay away from the evil sites

---

Gilgal (4:15). "This important Israelite sanctuary near Jericho was situated across the Jordan River from Baal Peor. From the time of the conquest, Gilgal was an important place of worship (Joshua 4:19–5:12; 1 Samuel 10:8; 11:12-15). Later in Israel's history, Gilgal became associated with wicked and syncretistic religious practices (Hosea 9:15; 12:11; Amos 4:4)."[2]

Beth Aven (4:15). "Literally, 'House of Idolatry' or 'Wickedness.' This was a contemptuous nickname for Bethel ('House of God'), the important royal sanctuary (Amos 4:4; 5:5; 7:13; 1 Kings 12:28-33)."[3]

Do not swear, "As surely as the Lord lives!" (4:15). "At these pagan sites . . . the name of

26

the Lord is not to be associated in any way with
such practices."[4]

5. In Hosea 5, what fault does God find with the
leaders of His people?

_they are unfaithful to God
their deed condemn them
so they cannot return to God_

6. How would you summarize the punishment
God promises for Israel and Judah in chapter 5?

_He will carry them off and not return
them until they admit guilt and seek
his face_

7. In your own words, express the response God is
seeking in chapter 5 from His people and their
rulers.

_God punishes his people for
unfaithfulness and with Israel
he destroyed them_

Mizpah . . . Tabor (5:1). "Mizpah in Gilead and
Tabor, a mountain in the Valley of Jezreel,
marked high points in Israel's past. Mizpah
was the home of Jephthah (Judges 10:17;
11:8,11,29,34), and Tabor was the scene of
Balak's victory (Judges 4:14; Tabor is also the
traditional site of the transfiguration)."[5]

Stumble (5:5). "Experience calamity (see Hosea
4:5)."[6]

8. In 5:12, God compares Himself to "moth" and "rot." Explain the appropriateness of these images in terms of the message God is communicating in this passage.

the moth destroys crops
rot destroys good food
and people

Ephraim turned to Assyria (5:13). "Assyrian records tell of the tribute paid to Tiglath-Pileser III by the Israelite kings Menarem and Hoshea (see 2 Kings 15:19-20; 17:3)."[7]

---

9. In 5:14, God compares Himself to a "lion" and a "great lion" (see also 11:10; 13:7-8). Again, explain the appropriateness of these images in their context.

Without the means of
God they will not
away or be consumed by
another conquror

10. What is most important in the people's response as expressed in Hosea 6:1-3?

if the people return to
God he will restore
them

Let us return (6:1). "Now the prophet includes himself in his imagining of humble submission to the Almighty's discipline. The Old Testament prophets did not separate themselves from the plight of their people (Isaiah 6:5; 53:4-6)."[8]

28

On the third day he will restore us (6:2). For this phrase, "the Septuagint's Greek translation . . . is part of what lay behind Jesus' and the New Testament writers' statements that Jesus' resurrection 'on the third day' was according to the Scriptures. Hosea was not writing about the Messiah directly, however, but about the people of Israel. The New Testament use of this idea depends on seeing a parallel between Israel's resurrection on the third day in this verse, and Jesus as the Messiah representing and embodying his people. The potential of Israel's third-day resurrection is to be ultimately realized in the resurrection of the One who acted in Israel's stead (see Matthew 3:13-15). This picture of Israel's death and resurrection thus sets the pattern for what eventually will be accomplished in and through Christ."[9]

For Further Study:
Hosea 6:2 speaks of a restoration that comes "on the third day," and this has been viewed as a foretelling or foreshadowing of the resurrection of Christ. What connections with this thought do you see in Jonah 1:17, Matthew 12:40, Luke 24:46, and 1 Corinthians 15:4?

Optional Application: How do the phrases expressed in Hosea 6:1-3 express faithfully the heart's desire that you and the people of your church possess? And how does this heart's desire translate into reality and action in your life?

Optional Application: Look again at Hosea 6:6, where the Lord states what He desires from His people. What does this mean in your own relationship with Him?

11. In 6:3, God is compared to "winter rains" and "spring rains." Explain the appropriateness of these images in terms of the message God is communicating in this passage.

If they return to God God will refresh them and return them to the good life they had before they sinned

12. In 6:4-7, how do you see God's character and the desire of His heart expressed?

God wants his people to acknowledge him and let him be the leader

13. According to 6:7-10, what are God's people guilty of?

they broke the covenant with God and became wicked and unfaithful acting like prostitutes and defiling Israel

29

For Further Study:
For the term *harvest* as symbolizing God's judgments, what do you discover in Jeremiah 51:33, Joel 3:13, Matthew 13:39-43, and Revelation 14:15?

Optional Application: What lessons about relying fully on God do you see in Hosea 7, and what do these mean for you personally in the particular challenges and responsibilities you face?

Gilead (6:8). This "is another of Hosea's allusions to former glories (Judges 10:17–11:11)."[10]

14. What significance do you see in the prophecy of 6:11?

a warning from God of the consequences of continuing to disobey God and to the reckoning that will take place.

Harvest (6:11). "A metaphor for God's judgment."[11] See also Hosea 8:7; 10:12-13.

15. In the rich and varied imagery in Hosea's words in chapter 7, which images stand out most strongly to you, and why?

How they sinned through deceit, thievery, adultery

16. In God's words as recorded in Hosea 7:1-7, what is emphasized about His people's sins?

wickedness and lies forgetting God in their passion of evil

17. What faults of God's people are revealed in 7:8-16?

arrogant, love God,
turns to other nations rather than turning to
God

I will throw my net over them (7:12). "The Lord
   himself was the hunter . . . and Israel was certain to be caught."[12]

---

18. How would you summarize the way Israel's
    apostasy is approached and dealt with in
    chapters 4–7?

19. In Hosea 4–7, what would you select as the key
    verse or passage—one that best captures or
    reflects the dynamics of what these chapters are
    all about?

20. What do these chapters in Hosea communicate
    most to you about the heart and character of
    God?

31

21. From what you see in these chapters, what does God especially want us to understand about the relationship He desires with His people?

_____

_____

_____

_____

22. List any lingering questions you have about Hosea 4–7.

_____

_____

_____

_____

_____

_____

For the group

Consider focusing your discussion for lesson 2 especially on some of the following issues, themes, and concepts recognized as major overall themes in Hosea. Which of these are dealt with in some way in chapters 4–7, and how are they further developed there?

- Human sinfulness
- Our repentance
- God's justice and judgment
- God's love
- God's uniqueness and holiness
- Apostasy and restoration

Questions 19–22 in lesson 2 are among those that may stimulate your best and most helpful discussion.

Remember to look also at the "For Thought and Discussion" questions in the margins.

1. *NIV Study Bible* (Grand Rapids, MI: Zondervan, 1985), at Hosea 4:3.
2. *New Geneva* (Nashville: Thomas Nelson, 1995), at Hosea 4:15.
3. *New Geneva*, at Hosea 4:15.
4. *ESV Study Bible* (Wheaton, IL: Crossway, 2008), at Hosea 4:15.
5. *ESV*, at Hosea 5:1.
6. *NIV*, at Hosea 5:5.
7. *NIV*, at Hosea 5:13.
8. *ESV*, at Hosea 6:1.
9. *ESV*, at Hosea 6:2.
10. *ESV*, at Hosea 6:8.
11. *New Geneva*, at Hosea 6:11.
12. *NIV*, at Hosea 7:12.

HOSEA 8–10

God's Punishment for His People

1. Proverbs 2:1-5 tells about the sincere person who truly longs for wisdom and understanding and searches the Scriptures for it as if there were treasure buried there. Such a person, this passage says, will come to understand the fear of the Lord and discover the knowledge of God. As you continue exploring the book of Hosea, what "hidden treasure" would you like God to help you find here—to show you what God and His wisdom are really like? If you have this desire, how would you express it in your own words of prayer to God?

For Thought and Discussion: How would you define *idolatry*, and to what extent is it something we should be aware of and understand?

_____

_____

_____

_____

2. Summarize the ways in which Israel's hypocrisy and apostasy are exposed in Hosea 8.

made idols of silver + gold

apostasy - take off on their own way

35

Trumpet . . . eagle (8:1). "The urgent call for alarm reports that Assyria, like an eagle, is rapidly approaching to administer God's judgment."[1]

We acknowledge you! (8:2). "Hosea . . . warns that sin can delude people into thinking that they know and understand God, when in fact they are far from Him."[2]

"The people practiced idolatrous forms of worship, but continued to call out to Yahweh, the God of Israel. This is the supreme irony. . . . The cold, hard fact was that he was not their God, and they were not his people. . . .

"They thought they knew God, but their knowledge was based only on history and tradition. It reminds us of the words of the Jews of Jesus' day, 'We are descendants of Abraham' (John 8:33). . . .

"The people who said they knew Yahweh were the same people who stole off to the gloomy groves where the laughter of prostitutes echoed. They performed acts of religious devotion to idols of stone; they gave their allegiance to grain and wine, and still expected God to act on their behalf. They did not know the ways of Yahweh. They knew better the ways of Baal."[3]

3. Note the question that is asked in the final line of Hosea 8:5. What do you see as the best answer to that question?

<u>Until they once again</u>
<u>accept God and return</u>

to him _[handwritten]_

For Thought and Discussion: Reflect further on the imagery in Hosea 8:7 of sowing the wind and reaping the whirlwind. What is the particular effectiveness and significance of this imagery?

depending on [handwritten] trying rather than God

Your calf-idol (8:5). "This calf-idol is reminiscent of the calf-idol made by Aaron (Exodus 32:1-4) and the calf-idol erected at Bethel (1 Kings 12:28-29)."[4]

Ephraim has sold herself to lovers (8:9). "The theme of spiritual adultery reappears at this point, for the nation is pictured as paying for lovers. Once again Hosea's marriage provides the catalyst for his message. However, her unfaithfulness is not idolatry in this context; it is her unlawful congress with Assyria. The allusion to hiring lovers can refer only to the massive tribute Israel had to pay to curry Assyrian favors."[5]

4. In 8:13-14, what significance do you see in the punishment God promises toward His people?

God will destroy them regardless of what fortification they place to save themselves _[handwritten]_

Return to Egypt (8:13). "God threatens them with captivity, here symbolized by the land where Israel earlier had been enslaved (Hosea 9:3; Exodus 1:8-14; Deuteronomy 28:68)."[6]

5. What are God's people warned about in Hosea 9:1-9, and what is the significance of these warnings?

Not to rejoice because they will be punish unless they stop their scanning worshiping idol _[handwritten]_

37

_____

_____

Bread of mourners (9:4). "Unclean, like bread in a
house where there had been a death (see Numbers
19:14; Deuteronomy 26:14; Jeremiah 16:7). All
who touched it became ceremonially unclean."[7]

They have sunk deep into corruption (9:9).
"Hosea's vivid depictions of sin remind
believers about the nature and consequences
of human sin."[8]

---

6. What are God's warnings—and their significance—in Hosea 9:10-17?

God hates them in their
practices and he will
drive them out of his house
they will suffer because
God will reject them

**When they came to Baal Peor . . . became as
vile as the thing they loved** (9:10). "People
become like the objects of their love."[9]

**Give them wombs that miscarry and breasts
that are dry** (9:14). "Hosea responds in
prayer. . . . The prophet can only agree with
God's righteous judgment."[10]

---

7. What is the portrait of Israel given in 10:1-2,
and what is being emphasized in those verses
about Israel and about God?

As Israel prospered
he built more altars and
adorned sacred stones;
deceitful.

8. What are the sins of God's people that He exposes in 10:3-6?

the people worship calf idols of Beth aven

9. What is the punishment God promises in 10:7-11?

disappear *Samaria will float away*
the high places will be destroyed
Thorns will cover the altars

no longer exist as a nation

They will say to the mountains, "Cover us!" and to the hills, "Fall on us!" (10:8). "Cries of utter despair; quoted by Jesus (Luke 23:30) and alluded to in Revelation 6:16 (see Isaiah 2:19)."[11]

---

10. In 10:12, what significance do you see in what God's people are asked to do?

God is asking the people to return to him and he will shower righteousness on them, repent

11. What is the punishment God promises in 10:13-15?

God will destroy Israel

Shalman devastated Beth Arbel (10:14). "Hosea's audience must have remembered this now unknown event as particularly brutal."[12] "Atrocities against civilians were common in ancient warfare (see Hosea 9:13; 13:16; 2 Kings 8:12-13; Psalm 137:8-9; Isaiah 13:16; Amos 1:13; Nahum 3:10)."[13]

12. How would you summarize the way Israel's apostasy is approached and dealt with in chapters 8–10?

> Because of their sins and falling away from him God threatens to destroy Israel as a people

*no pregnancy
no conception
their children slayed*

13. In Hosea 8–10, what would you select as the key verse or passage—one that best captures or reflects the dynamics of what these chapters are all about?

> ✓ 8-1 God warns Israel in
> v 5 to destroy their idols
> ✓ 10 God will save them
> by destroying their idols

14. What do these chapters in Hosea communicate most to you about the heart and character of God?

> God will punish when the people deviate from his teachings

15. From what you see in these chapters, what does God especially want us to understand about the relationship He desires with His people?

That his people love him
and obey his commands

16. List any lingering questions you have about Hosea 8–10.

For the group

Consider focusing your discussion for lesson 3 especially on some of the following issues, themes, and concepts recognized as major overall themes in Hosea. Which of these are dealt with in some way in chapters 8–10, and how are they further developed there?

- Human sinfulness
- Our repentance
- God's justice and judgment
- God's love
- God's uniqueness and holiness
- Apostasy and restoration

   Questions 13–16 in lesson 3 are among those that may stimulate your best and most helpful discussion.
   Remember to look also at the "For Thought and Discussion" questions in the margins.

1. *New Geneva* (Nashville: Thomas Nelson, 1995), at Hosea 8:1.
2. *New Geneva*, introduction to Hosea, "Characteristics and Themes."

3. Thomas Edward McComiskey, "Hosea," *The Minor Prophets* (Grand Rapids, MI: Baker, 2009), 120–121.

4. *ESV Study Bible* (Wheaton, IL: Crossway, 2008), at Hosea 8:5-6.

5. McComiskey, 129.

6. *New Geneva*, at Hosea 8:13.

7. *NIV Study Bible* (Grand Rapids, MI: Zondervan, 1985), at Hosea 9:4.

8. *New Geneva*, introduction to Hosea.

9. *New Geneva*, introduction to Hosea.

10. *New Geneva*, at Hosea 9:14.

11. *NIV*, at Hosea 10:8.

12. *New Geneva*, at Hosea 10:14.

13. *NIV*, at Hosea 10:14.

HOSEA 11–14

God's Everlasting Love for His People

next 5 pages

"The atmosphere changes here. We leave behind the tumult of war and the slaughter of innocents to move back through time to the halcyon period of Israel's early history. It was a time marked by the greatest event in her national experience — the exodus from Egypt. Hosea pictures Israel in this period as an infant, dependent on an adult for care and training."[1]

"In language even more tender than the story of the prodigal son (Luke 15:11-32), God, the loving parent, proclaims His compassion for Israel. In spite of rebellion, God's election cannot be defeated. Beyond judgment there is hope."[2]

1. How are God's actions toward His people portrayed in Hosea 11:1-4, and what do they reveal about His heart and character?

_____

For Thought and Discussion: From what you're seeing in Hosea, what does God want His people to learn most in this book about His love for them?

he lifted the yoke

For Further Study: What more do you learn about Israel as God's "son" and the Lord as Israel's "Father" in Exodus 4:22-23, Deuteronomy 32:6, Isaiah 1:2-4, and Jeremiah 2:14?

beginning as a child, a son but went far from God the more they worshiped Baals even as God healed them and was kind to them

When Israel was a child, I loved him (11:1). This book of Hosea "presents God's relationship to his people as a divine-human love story."[3]

Out of Egypt I called my son (11:1). "Matthew found in the call of Israel from Egypt a typological picture of Jesus' coming from Egypt (see Matthew 2:15).[4] "Matthew 2:15 uses the line . . . to show that Jesus is the 'Son of God,' i.e., the heir of David who embodies Israel's relationship to God (see 2 Samuel 7:14; Psalm 89:26-27)."[5]

2. What is the punishment against His people that God promises in 11:5-7, and for what reason?

they will return to Egypt because they refuse to repent their cities will be destroyed, God will no longer exalt them

3. In 11:8-9, what is most significant to you in what God says about Himself and His people?

God does not want to give them up, he will not come to them in wrath

Admah . . . Zeboyim (11:8). "Cities of the plain (Genesis 10:19; 14:2,8), overthrown when Sodom was destroyed (Genesis 19:24-25; Deuteronomy 29:23; Jeremiah 49:18) and symbolizing total destruction."[6]

44

4. Why do you think the Lord emphasizes in 11:9 that He is "God, and not a man"?

He does not act like men in anger and comes wrath, like children when God calls they will come

Optional Application: In what ways does the story told in Hosea 11:1-11 match your own experience with the Lord God and His dealings with you?

5. What future is prophesied for Israel in 11:10-11?

they will flee from Egypt and run to God to be settled by the Lord in Israel

6. What is the significance of the way Judah is singled out in 11:12?

Judah is unruly against God even to the Holy One

7. What is the significance of how Israel (Ephraim) is described in 12:1?

Ephraim feeds on the West Wind, lies and makes treaties with Assyria and trades with Egypt   violence

8. What further accusations does the Lord make against His people in 12:2-14?

Judah Ephraim grasped in prophecies head as he Struggled with God, and an angel who to beg for his favor, us sacrificed bulls in Gilgal

Optional Application: In the Lord's commands to His people in Hosea 12:6, what personal message do you hear from Him for your own life at this time? What do these words communicate about the kind of relationship your heavenly Father desires with you?

For Further Study: For further background on the life of Jacob as mentioned in Hosea 12, read Genesis 25:26; 28:2-5; 29:20,28; 32:24-31; 35:9-15. What do you discover in these passages?

Optional Application: In Hosea 12:9 and 13:4, the Lord declares, "I have been the LORD your God." In a fresh way, reflect on the personal significance of this statement. What does it mean most for you that He is the Lord your God?

9. What are the most important aspects of the man Jacob's life mentioned in 12:3-4 and 12:12, and how do they link with Hosea's message in this chapter?

struggled with God and struggled and overcame an Angel and begged for his favor served to get a wife in dream

10. What is revealed about the Lord's heart and character in 12:2-14?

_God will punish v 2
God will forgive v6
God will punish the unfaithful v 9
God will repay unfaithfulness with contempt_

---

*The LORD **used a prophet to bring Israel up from Egypt, by a prophet he cared for him*** (12:13). "The first prophet is clearly Moses (Deuteronomy 18:15; 34:10-12) and the second probably is as well. The preserving prophet could, however, be a later prophet such as Samuel (Jeremiah 15:1) or Elijah (1 Kings 19:9-18)."[7]

---

11. Summarize the contrasting pictures of God and man-made gods as presented in 13:1-8.

those who worship idols will be like the morning mist those that worship God will be cared for through all adversity.

When Ephraim spoke, people trembled (13:1). "The idea seems to be that at one time Ephraim's word commanded respect."[8]

He was exalted in Israel (13:1). "In accordance
with Jacob's blessing (Genesis 48:10-20),
Ephraim became a powerful tribe (Judges 8:1-3;
12:1-7; 1 Samuel 1:1-4), from which came such
prominent leaders as Joshua (Joshua 24:30) and
Jeroboam I (1 Kings 11:26; 12:20)."[9]

12. Recall 5:14 and 11:10, where God is compared
to a lion. In 13:7-8, the Lord says that He is
"like a lion" and "like a leopard" and "like a bear
robbed of her cubs." Explain the appropriateness of these images in light of the message
God is communicating here in chapter 13.

God is a loving God
but will not accept falling away
after saving you - he will let
one suffer as they wish when they
fall away

13. In what ways is God's judgment against His
people portrayed in 13:9-16?

God will leave them to their
evil desires until they
repent of this evil

***In my anger I gave you a king, and in my wrath
I took him away*** (13:11). These statements
"may be a reference to Saul, the first king of
Israel; Israel asked for the wrong kind of king
(1 Samuel 8:4-9), and still does."[10]

***I will deliver this people from the power of
the grave; I will redeem them from death***
(13:14). Or as questions: "Shall I ransom them
from the power of Sheol? Shall I redeem them
from Death?" (ESV). "In the Old Testament,
'Sheol' is a proper name and can be a poetic
personification of the grave (for example, 1
Kings 2:6; Psalm 141:7). But it can also desig-
nate the grim destination of the wicked after

death (for example, Psalm 49:14-15). The parallel wording with Psalm 49:15 suggests that Hosea sees Ephraim's 'death' as leading to Sheol in the second sense, i.e., as damnation. Thus God asks himself whether he should rescue Ephraim from such consequences."[11]

Where, O death, are your plagues? Where, O grave, is your destruction? (13:14). "This verse is one of the great Old Testament affirmations of God's power over the last enemy, death (compare 1 Corinthians 15:55). Whereas the old Israel of Hosea's time did not avail itself of the divine power over death, the true spiritual Israel (Christ with His church) experiences it. Final triumph over God's last enemy is assured by the death of Christ and His resurrection from the grave."[12]

"As we move toward the conclusion of Hosea's prophecy, the thundering voice of the prophet becomes a tender whisper as he pleads lovingly with Israel. Hosea must have pleaded in the same way with Gomer when he bought her from her paramour (chapter 3). He had besought her to return with him to their home and establish a new relationship. Now Hosea calls on Israel to leave her lovers and come to God in repentance."[13]

14. Summarize what the Lord asks His people to do in Hosea 14 and what He promises to do for them.

return to Hem

_____

_____

_____

48

Take words with you (14:2). This phrase means "to know ahead of time what you will say."[14] "Only words of true repentance would be sufficient."[15] "The key to survival and eventual exaltation as a people was simple, yet profound. They had only to take with them words and acknowledge their wrongdoing. If their hearts were broken, their relationship to God would be mended."[16]

(handwritten margin note: pray / forgiveness)

In you the fatherless find compassion (14:3). "This alludes to the earlier theme of loss and restoration of love illustrated by Hosea's marriage and his daughter Lo-Ruhamah [No Mercy] (Hosea 1:6; 2:2-4,14-23)."[17]

15. In 14:8, God compares Himself to "a flourishing juniper." Explain the appropriateness of this image in light of the overall message God is communicating here.

God can make one fruitful

Flourishing juniper (14:8). Also translated as "evergreen cypress" (ESV) or "luxuriant cypress" (NASB). "A tree renowned as a symbol of life";[18] "ever full of life and strength."[19]

16. What significance do you see in the final verse of this book?

If you believe and walk with God he will be faithful and keep you on the right path

Optional Application: Here again is our heavenly Father's gracious invitation in Hosea 14:2: "Take words with you and return to the LORD. Say to him: 'Forgive all our sins and receive us graciously, that we may offer the fruit of our lips.'" What are the words you would like to take with you as you draw near to the Lord at this time?

Optional Application: What personal comfort and hope do you find in the final line of Hosea 14:3?

Optional
Application: Look
again at the final
verse in Hosea, espe-
cially its questions:
"Who is wise? . . . Who
is discerning?" What
wisdom and discern-
ment has God given
you? How does it
connect with what
is being taught in
Hosea 14:9?

*The ways of the LORD are right; the righteous
walk in them, but the rebellious stumble
in them* (14:9). "The ways of God are free of
obstacles for the righteous. . . . What God has
instituted is for our good. We find satisfaction
and nobility in a life that is lived humbly before
God. Those who rebel against God's yoke will
stumble over his commands; they will find his
strictures too hard to bear."[20]

17. In Hosea 11–14, what would you select as the
key verse or passage—one that best captures or
reflects the dynamics of what these chapters are
all about? *13 Vs 4*

    *But I am the Lord your
    God who brought you out
    of Egypt you shall have
    no God but me*

18. What do these chapters in Hosea communicate
most to you about the heart and character of
God?

    *We have a loving God
    who punishes unrighteousness
    and like a father will
    not drive us away because
    we sin*

    but forgives

19. List any lingering questions you have about
Hosea 11–14.

Reviewing the book of Hosea

20. In your study of the book of Hosea, what have you learned and appreciated most?

God is our Lord and God is loving and compassionate if we believe; is forgiving
Hope

21. In Isaiah 55:10-11, God reminds us that in the same way He sends rain and snow from the sky to water the earth and nurture life, He sends His words to accomplish specific purposes. What would you suggest are God's primary purposes for the message of Hosea in the lives of His people today?

Gods word will still save sometimes it takes a while but the words will save anyone willing to listen

22. Review the guidelines given for our thought-life in Philippians 4:8 — "Whatever is true, whatever is noble, whatever is right, whatever is pure, whatever is lovely, whatever is admirable — if anything is excellent or praiseworthy — *think about such things*" (emphasis added). As you reflect on all you've read in this book of Hosea, what stands out to you as being particularly *true*, or *noble*, or *right*, or *pure*, or *lovely*, or *admirable*, or *excellent*, or *praiseworthy* — and therefore well worth thinking more about?

Gods love + forgiveness

If we read the bible and consider what we have read our message will be apparent if will think about it sometimes it take little thinking but sometimes we need to spend more time on what we read

Optional Application: Which verses in Hosea would be most helpful for you to memorize so you have them always available in your mind and heart for the Holy Spirit to use?

23. Considering that all of Scripture testifies ultimately of Christ, where does *Jesus* come most in focus for you in this book?

14 — thru 7

Dwell in his shade

and flourish

24. What are the strongest ways Hosea points us to mankind's need for Jesus and what He accomplished in His death and resurrection?

14 — v 8

leave your idols and

return to God

25. In Romans 15:4, Paul reminds us that the Old Testament Scriptures can give us patience and perseverance on one hand, as well as comfort and encouragement on the other. In your own life, how do you see the book of Hosea living up to Paul's description? In what ways do the Old Testament Scriptures help meet your personal need for both perseverance and encouragement?

Offers a means of

communicating with

God.

For the group

Consider focusing your discussion for lesson 4 especially on some of the following issues, themes, and concepts recognized as major overall themes in Hosea. Which of these are dealt with in some way in chapters 11–14, and how are they further developed there?

- Human sinfulness
- Our repentance
- God's justice and judgment
- God's love
- God's uniqueness and holiness
- Apostasy and restoration

Questions 17–19 in lesson 4 are among those that may stimulate your best and most helpful discussion.

Also, allow enough discussion time to look back together and review all of Hosea as a whole. You can use the numbered questions 20–25 in this lesson to help you do that.

Look also at the question in the margin under the heading "For Thought and Discussion."

1. Thomas Edward McComiskey, "Hosea," *The Minor Prophets* (Grand Rapids, MI: Baker, 2009), 184.
2. *New Geneva Study Bible* (Nashville: Thomas Nelson, 1995), at Hosea 11:1-11.
3. Leland Ryken and Philip Graham Ryken, eds., introduction to Hosea, "The book of Hosea as a chapter in the master story of the Bible," *The Literary Study Bible* (Wheaton, IL: Crossway, 2007).
4. *NIV Study Bible* (Grand Rapids, MI: Zondervan, 1985), at Hosea 11:1.
5. *ESV Study Bible* (Wheaton, IL: Crossway, 2008), at Hosea 11:1.
6. *NIV*, at Hosea 11:8.
7. *New Geneva*, at Hosea 12:13.
8. *ESV*, at Hosea 13:1.
9. *NIV*, at Hosea 13:1.
10. *ESV*, at Hosea 13:11.
11. *ESV*, at Hosea 13:14.
12. *New Geneva*, at Hosea 13:14.
13. McComiskey, 229.
14. *ESV*, at Hosea 14:2.
15. *NIV*, at Hosea 14:2.
16. McComiskey, 237.
17. *New Geneva*, at Hosea 14:3.
18. *New Geneva*, at Hosea 14:8.
19. *ESV*, at Hosea 14:8.
20. McComiskey, 237.

JOEL

A Warning of Judgment

"The central message of the Book of Joel concerns the coming day of the Lord. Joel introduces that day in the context of the then-present destruction of the land's vegetation, a destruction that was a sign of judgment against the covenant community. Only their return to God would avert the imminent day of the Lord that would 'come as destruction from the Almighty' (1:15). . . .

"The church has continued to find the teaching in the Book of Joel on the day of the Lord to be an important source of hope and comfort on the one hand, and a word of warning on the other."[1]

"We remember the book of Joel for its motif of the attack of the killer locusts. We infer that Joel's prophecy was occasioned by a plague of locusts that engulfed Judah. In Joel's prophetic imagination, the locusts become amplified into images of horror — pictures of God's judgment against human sinfulness. Of course Joel's images are timeless and universal, and so is the horror that the book evokes regarding God's punishment of human evil."[2]

This book "contains no clear indications of when it was written. . . . Some scholars date the book in the ninth century B.C., and others in the period just prior to the Jewish exile in Babylon during the sixth century B.C. But most scholars now prefer a date following this exile. . . . There is good reason to conclude . . . that the date of the book simply cannot be known with certainty."[3]

"Several features suggest that the Book of Joel as a whole is either a liturgical text intended for repeated use on occasions of national lament or at least a historical example of one such lament. . . . This feature of the book may help explain not only why it is so difficult to date, but also how it achieves the kind of timelessness that makes it such powerful literature in our own day."[4]

1. In Jeremiah 23:29, God says that His Word is "like fire" and "like a hammer." He can use the Scriptures to burn away unclean thoughts and desires in our hearts. He can also use Scripture, with hammer-like hardness, to crush and crumble our spiritual hardness. From your study of Joel, how do you most want to see the fire-and-hammer power of God's Word at work

in your own life? Express this longing in a written prayer to God.

bringing his people both
to him

2. In Joel 1:1-12, what do you see as the strongest imagery and statements in this description of the locust invasion?

Vs 5-7 A nation has invaded
my land, laid waste my vines
ruined my fig trees

Left . . . eaten . . . left . . . eaten . . . left . . .
eaten (1:4). "The poetic repetitions in every line emphasize the thoroughness of the locusts' destruction."[5]

"It is difficult for modern Western people to appreciate the dire threat represented by a locust plague in earlier periods. Such outbreaks had serious consequences for the health and mortality of an affected population and for a region's economy. Scarcity of food resulting from the swarm's attack would bring the population to subsistence intake or less, would make the spread of disease among a weakened populace easier, would eliminate any trade from surplus food products, and would stimulate high inflation in the costs of food products.

For Thought and Discussion: How familiar is the book of Joel to you? What have been your previous impressions of this book?

Optional Application: After His resurrection, when Jesus was explaining Old Testament passages to His disciples, we read that He "opened their minds so they could understand the Scriptures" (Luke 24:45). Ask God to do that kind of work in *your* mind as you study the book of Joel so you're released and free to learn everything here He wants you to learn and so you can become as bold, worshipful, and faithful as those early disciples of Jesus. Express this desire to Him in prayer.

57

For Further Study:
Notice in Solomon's prayer of dedication for the temple how he spoke of what the people should do in a time of locust invasion (see 2 Chronicles 6:28-31). How well does the book of Joel follow those guidelines?

See also the Lord's response to Solomon concerning such situations (see 2 Chronicles 7:13-14) and His instructions there. How well does the book of Joel follow the pattern set out there?

For Further Study:
Review what God calls His people to do in Joel 1:13-14. How does this compare with what the people of Nineveh did as recorded in Jonah 3:5-8?

For Thought and Discussion: What does the phrase "the day of the LORD" mean to you?

Disease outbreaks are further aggravated when swarms die; the putrefaction of the millions of locust bodies breeds typhus and other diseases that spread to humans and animals."[6]

3. What is most significant in the request God makes to His people in 1:13-14?

Summon the elders and all who live in the land to the house of the Lord and cry out to to the house

All who live in the land (1:14). "The call to repentance is given not merely to a select number of the covenant community, but rather to all the Lord's people who are called to return to Him: young and old, men and women, leaders and followers, and even those who might otherwise be exempted from community responsibilities (nursing mothers and newlyweds, 1:13-14; 2:15-17).

4. In 1:15-20, what do you see as the strongest imagery and statements in this description of the "day of the LORD"?

V 19-20

The day of the LORD (1:15). See also verses 1, 11, and 31 in chapter 2 and verse 14 in chapter 3.

"Joel ... moves quickly from an accurate description of a real devastation by locusts in chapter 1 to a description of the dreadful locust-like army of the Lord that blends the literal and figurative in chapter 2. It seems then that the destruction by locusts that Joel had seen became the vehicle for his prophecy proclaiming the need to repent in view of the coming day of the Lord."[7]

For Further Study: Reflect on the repeated theme in Joel of "the day of the Lord" (1:15; 2:1,11,31; 3:14). Compare this with the prophecies concerning the "day of the Lord" in these passages: Isaiah 2:12-21; 13:6-13; Jeremiah 46:10; Ezekiel 7:10-14; Amos 5:18-20; 8:9-10; Obadiah 15; Zephaniah 1:7,14-16; Malachi 4:5.

5. In 2:1-11, what do you see as the strongest imagery and statements in this further description of the "day of the Lord"?

   V 7   they charge like
   warriors, scale walls like soldiers
   plunge through defenses without
   breaking ranks

For Further Study: How does the prophet's pronouncement of God's coming day of destruction in Joel 1:15 compare with Jonah's God-given message to Nineveh in Jonah 3:4?

6. What is most significant in the request God makes to His people in 2:12-17?

   V-12: return to me with all
   your heart with fasting +
   weeping and mourning
   return to the Lord

Return to me with all your heart (2:12). "The return to God that Joel calls for involves the whole person. Such repentance is to be manifested externally through such actions as mourning, weeping, crying out to the Lord, and fasting. But merely external or ritual manifestations of repentance are not adequate, and the Lord calls the people to show the sincerity of their repentance."[8]

Optional Application: In the words of the Lord to His people in Joel 2:12-13 (a call to repentance), what is His particular message for you at this moment in your life?

For Further Study: For background to the words in Joel 2:13 about God's loving character, see God's words to Moses in Exodus 34:6. (See also Psalm 86:5,15; 103:8; 145:8.)

For Further Study: How does the question in Joel 2:14 compare with the words spoken by the king in Nineveh as recorded in Jonah 3:9?

He is gracious and compassionate, slow to anger and abounding in love (2:13). "Motivation for repentance lies firmly in the nature of God."[9]

---

7. What promises from God do you see in 2:18-27?

He will take pity on his people sending grain, new wine, + oil and never again will I make you an object of scorn

8. What does 2:18-27 communicate most about God's heart and character?

_____

_____

_____

_____

9. What special significance do you see in the promise God states in 2:25? (Refer to Joel 1:4.)

_____

_____

_____

_____

Enough to satisfy you fully . . . plenty to eat (2:19,26). "God is concerned . . . that his people have plenty."[10]

---

10. What further promises from God do you see in 2:28-32, and what is their significance?

_____

_____

_____

_____

In the first part of Joel, the "day of the Lord" was depicted as a day of terrible judgment. "However, in the second part of the book, Joel introduces a second prophetic tradition about the day of the Lord, namely, that the day of the Lord is a day of judgment against the enemies of His people, whom he will protect and bless (Ezekiel 25–32; Jeremiah 46–51; Isaiah 13). On the day of the Lord, the nations will be accountable for their crimes against the Lord's people and will be judged accordingly (Joel 3:2-16,19). But the people of the Lord's inheritance will enjoy His protection and be spiritually and physically blessed (Joel 2:28-32; 3:16-18,20,21)."[11]

11. What promises from God regarding other nations do you see in Joel 3:1-8?

_____

_____

_____

_____

12. How would you summarize the thrust and emphasis in the prophetic words of 3:9-16?

_____

_____

_____

_____

For Further Study: In the New Testament, how do you see Joel 2:28-32 being fulfilled and referred to in Acts 2?

For Further Study: How does the imagery of Joel 2:30 reappear — and receive further development — in the words of Jesus as recorded in Matthew 24:29-31; Mark 13:24-27; Luke 21:10-19,25-28; and Revelation 9:2?

For Further Study: Reflect on the salvation truth proclaimed in the first half of Joel 2:32. What role does this truth play in the teaching of the apostle Paul in Romans 10:9-13? How is this truth also expanded and deepened in Psalm 50:15 and 1 Corinthians 1:2?

Optional Application: What does it mean for you personally to be someone "who calls on the name of the LORD" (Joel 2:32)? What does it truly mean for you to call on His name?

Optional Application: How do the words of Joel 3:16 link and relate to your own perspective of God? In what ways do you desire to understand more fully this perspective of Him?

13. What further promises from God are made in Joel 3:17-21, and what is their significance?

_____

_____

_____

_____

14. What have you learned in this book about the biblical concept of "the day of the LORD"?

_____

_____

_____

_____

15. What have you learned most or appreciated most in your study of the book of Joel?

_____

_____

_____

_____

16. In this book of Joel, what would you select as the key verse or passage—one that best captures or reflects the dynamics of what the book is all about?

_____

_____

_____

_____

17. What does the book of Joel communicate most to you about the heart and character of God?

_____

_____

_____

_____

18. List any lingering questions you have about the book of Joel.

_____

_____

_____

_____

19. Recall again the words of Isaiah 55:10-11, where God reminds us that in the same way He sends rain and snow from the sky to water the earth and nurture life, He sends His words to accomplish specific purposes. What would you suggest are God's primary purposes for the message of Joel in the lives of His people today?

_____

_____

_____

_____

20. Review again the guidelines given for our thought-life in Philippians 4:8 — "Whatever is true, whatever is noble, whatever is right, whatever is pure, whatever is lovely, whatever is admirable — if anything is excellent or praise-worthy — *think about such things*" (emphasis added). As you reflect on all you've read in this book of Joel, what stands out to you as being particularly *true,* or *noble,* or *right,* or *pure,* or *lovely,* or *admirable,* or *excellent,* or *praise-worthy* — and therefore well worth thinking more about?

_____

_____

_____

_____

Optional Application: Which verse or verses in the book of Joel would be most helpful for you to memorize so you have them always available in your mind and heart for the Holy Spirit to use?

21. Considering that all of Scripture testifies ultimately of Christ, where does Jesus come most in focus for you in this book?

22. In your understanding, what are the strongest ways Joel points us to mankind's need for Jesus and what He accomplished in His death and resurrection?

23. Recall again Paul's words in Romans 15:4, reminding us that the Old Testament Scriptures can give us patience, perseverance, comfort, and encouragement. In your own life, how do you see the book of Joel living up to Paul's description? In what ways do the Old Testament Scriptures help meet your personal need for both perseverance and encouragement?

For the group

Consider focusing your discussion for lesson 5 especially on the following issues, themes, and concepts recognized as major overall themes in Joel. How do you see these being dealt with in this book?

- God's judgment
- Repentance and restoration
- Redemption and salvation
- The "day of the LORD"

Questions 14–23 in lesson 5 are among those that may stimulate your best and most helpful discussion.

Look also at the questions in the margins under the heading "For Thought and Discussion."

1. *New Geneva Study Bible*, introduction to Joel, "Characteristics and Themes" (Nashville: Thomas Nelson, 1995).
2. Leland Ryken and Philip Graham Ryken, eds., introduction to Joel, "The Book at a Glance," *The Literary Study Bible* (Wheaton, IL: Crossway, 2007).
3. *New Geneva*, introduction to Joel, "Date and Occasion."
4. Raymond Bryan Dillard, "Joel," *The Minor Prophets*, ed. Thomas Edward McComiskey (Grand Rapids, MI: Baker, 2009), 243–244.
5. *New Geneva*, at Joel 1:4.
6. Dillard, 255–256.
7. *New Geneva*, introduction to Joel.
8. *New Geneva*, introduction to Joel.
9. *New Geneva*, introduction to Joel.
10. Dillard, 292.
11. *New Geneva*, introduction to Joel.

AMOS 1–2

An Announcement of Judgment

"The prophecy of Amos covers so much territory, and with such a range of prophetic techniques and motifs, that it is in effect a minianthology of prophetic writings. . . . The prophet himself emerges as one of the most forceful characters in the Bible, so that we feel as though he is one of our closest acquaintances."[1]

"The prophecies of Amos . . . are closely related to those of Hosea. Their ministries were different, however, in that Hosea was a native of the Northern Kingdom, and Amos was a Judean who journeyed to Israel to prophesy. . . . Amos was sent by the Lord to pronounce judgment upon the rebellious people of Israel."[2]

"The prophet Amos came from Tekoa (1:1), a village some ten miles south of Jerusalem and six miles south of Bethlehem in Judah. Amos probably grew up in Tekoa, and learned there the related skills of a shepherd (1:1) and a livestock breeder (7:14). His work must have required him to travel, however, because he was also a dresser of sycamore-fig trees (7:14), which are not found more than one thousand feet above sea level and grow nowhere near Tekoa (which lies over two thousand feet above sea level), but in the lower lands of the Jordan Valley and on the shores of the Dead Sea and the Mediterranean. Moreover, Tekoa is only a day's journey from Samaria, and it is possible that Amos pursued his various callings in the north as well as the south. . . .

"Amos had not studied to be a prophet (7:14) . . . but the Lord sovereignly called him to be one. Amos ministered primarily to the northern kingdom (7:15), although his prophecies also addressed the sins of Judah (2:4-5; compare 9:11)."[3]

1. In Jeremiah 23:29, God says that His Word is "like fire" and "like a hammer." He can use the Scriptures to burn away unclean thoughts and desires in our hearts. He can also use Scripture, with hammer-like hardness, to crush and crumble our spiritual hardness. From your study of Amos, how do you most want to see the fire-and-hammer power of God's Word at work in your life? Express this longing in a written prayer to God.

_____

_____

_____

_____

2. What do you know already about the kings mentioned in Amos 1:1?

Sinful kings

Earthquake (1:1). "This earthquake was a memorable event in an earthquake-prone region. It was remembered as an act of divine judgment in Zechariah 14:5 ('you shall flee as you fled from the earthquake in the days of King Uzziah of Judah'). A date around 760 B.C. has been proposed." [4]

3. What is being emphasized in verse 2 of this first chapter? How does this verse set the stage for what follows?

Illustrates the power of God over events

4. Summarize God's judgment against Damascus (Syria) as given in 1:3-5.

He will destroy the fortress of Ben Hadad and destroy the king in the valley of Aven and send the people into exile

For three sins . . . even for four (1:3). Equivalent to "for their many sins, especially the one named." [5] See this also in verses 6, 9, 11, and 13 in chapter 1 and in verses 1, 4, and 6 in chapter 2. "This poetic expression is used to introduce

Optional Application: We read that after Jesus' resurrection, when He was explaining Old Testament passages to His disciples, He "opened their minds so they could understand the Scriptures" (Luke 24:45). Ask God to do that kind of work in *your* mind as you study the book of Amos so you're released and free to learn everything here He wants you to learn and so you can become as bold, worshipful, and faithful as those early disciples of Jesus. Express this desire to Him in prayer.

For Thought and Discussion: How familiar is the book of Amos to you? What have been your previous impressions of this book?

For Further Study: For more background on the kings mentioned in Amos 1:1, see 2 Kings 15:1-7 and 2 Chronicles 26:6-23 (for Uzziah; also known as Azariah); and 2 Kings 14:23-29 (for Jeroboam son of Joash).

Optional Application: If God said concerning *you*, "For three sins . . . even for four," what might those sins be? How has God dealt with those sins through the cross of Christ? What victory over those sins has Christ won for you and brought to you?

For Thought and Discussion: In the opening chapters of Amos, what do these various judgments against the nations imply and assume about God's authority over the peoples and nations of the world?

the judgment upon all seven of the neighboring nations, and upon Israel as well (2:6). It is a way of expressing totality: 'three' expresses the plural in Hebrew, and by raising it to 'four' the idea of multiplicity is conveyed."[6]

I will not relent (1:3). Or "I will not revoke its punishment" (NASB); "I will not revoke the punishment" (ESV); "I will not turn away its punishment" (NKJV).

5. Summarize God's judgment against Gaza (the Philistines) as given in 1:6-8.

> God will totally destroy
> the people of Gaza

6. Summarize God's judgment against Tyre as given in 1:9-10.

> God will destroy tyre
> because of the sins
> committed — selling
> communities into captivity

7. Summarize God's judgment against Edom as given in 1:11-12.

> God punishment is
> fierce for going against
> his advice

8. Summarize God's judgment against Ammon as given in 1:13-15.

> God will punish those
> who go against his will

"Sovereign over the world, Amos's God is also the Lord of the nations. As Lord he is also Judge. He can, and does, raise up one nation against another in judgment — a process that will continue until the Lord's return (for he is now, as always, 'the Judge of all the earth,' Genesis 18:25)."[7]

For Further Study:
As you reflect on God's judgments against the nations as set forth in Amos 1 and 2, describe what background support for such judgments you find in the following passages: Deuteronomy 32:8; Psalm 67:4; 82:8; 94:2; 96:10; 115:16; Acts 17:26.

For Further Study:
What connections do you see between the prophecy concerning Judah in Amos 2:4-5 and Ezekiel 7:20-22, 8:6, and 11:22-23?

9. Summarize God's judgment against Moab as given in Amos 2:1-3.

He will totally destroy moab

10. Summarize God's judgment against Judah as given in 2:4-5.

God does punish for sins and for rejecting is laws and decrees

---

I will send fire on Judah that will consume the fortresses of Jerusalem (2:5). "Over 150 years after Amos's prophecy, Nebuchadnezzar II conquered Jerusalem and fulfilled this prophecy."[8] See 2 Kings 25:8-10; Jeremiah 39:8.

"The Lord's indictment now turns, no doubt unexpectedly, against Israel. The

71

For Further Study:
In Numbers 6 and
Jeremiah 35, what do
you learn about the
Nazirites?

Israelites might have thought the mighty
poem complete, with the seventh oracle
against Judah delivering the ultimate blast
against a rival nation. But it was not so....
A series of indictments come forth."[9]

11. Summarize God's judgment against Israel as
    given in 2:6-8.

    They sell righteousness for silver
    and the needy for a pair of sandals
    they profane God holyname
    through adultry

12. What actions on God's part does He mention in
    2:9-11, and what do these tell us about the Lord
    and His grace and mercy toward His people?

    He lead them out of
    Egypt, destroyed the Amorites
    led them for 40 years and gave
    them the land of the amorites

but they corrupted
God plan for them

13. What is the significance of what the people do
    in 2:12?

    they corrupted Gods plan
    for them

14. What further judgment from God against Israel
    is promised in 2:13-16?

    God will crush them
    and they will not escape
    and no one will be able
    to stand against God

72

15. In these first two chapters of the book of Amos, what would you select as the key verse or passage—one that best captures or reflects the dynamics of what these chapters are all about?

✓ 2-13

16. What do these chapters in Amos communicate most to you about the heart and character of God?

every one a drama & warning

17. List any lingering questions you have about Amos 1–2.

For the group

Consider focusing your discussion for lesson 6 especially on some of the following issues, themes, and concepts recognized as major overall themes in Amos. Which of these are dealt with in some way in chapters 1–2, and how are they further developed there?

- Moral and ethical responsibility of individuals and societies
- Sin
- God's judgment
- God's blessing, restoration, and salvation

Questions 15–17 in lesson 6 are among those that may stimulate your best and most helpful discussion.

Remember to look also at the "For Thought and Discussion" questions in the margins.

1. Leland Ryken and Philip Graham Ryken, eds., introduction to Amos, "The Book at a Glance," *The Literary Study Bible* (Wheaton, IL: Crossway, 2007).
2. Warren Baker, ed., *The Complete Word Study Old Testament* (Chattanooga, TN: AMG Publishers, 1994), introduction to Hosea.
3. Jeff Niehaus, "Amos," *The Minor Prophets*, ed. Thomas Edward McComiskey (Grand Rapids, MI: Baker, 2009), 315–316.
4. Niehaus, 336.
5. *NIV Study Bible* (Grand Rapids, MI: Zondervan, 1985), at Amos 1:3.
6. *ESV Study Bible* (Wheaton, IL: Crossway, 2008), at Amos 1:3.
7. Niehaus, 326.
8. Niehaus, 362.
9. Niehaus, 365.

AMOS 3–6

Reasons for Judgment

1. Recall again the message of Proverbs 2:1-5 about the sincere person who searches the Scriptures as if there were treasure buried there. As you continue exploring the book of Amos, what "hidden treasure" would you like God to help you find here to show you what God and His wisdom are really like? If you have this desire, express it in your own words of prayer to God.

_____

_____

_____

_____

2. a. In Amos 3:1-6, what is the line of reasoning that the Lord develops in these words of admonishment to His people Israel?

_____

_____

_____

_____

b. What is the answer to each of the questions asked in 3:3-6?

_____

_____

For Thought and Discussion: In Amos 3:2, God says that specifically because He lovingly chose Israel He is punishing her. In this kind of relationship, why is such discipline a necessary element?

For Further Study: What connections do you see between Amos 3:7 and Isaiah 44:26?

_____

_____

Chosen (3:2). Or "known" (ESV, NKJV). "In addition to cognition (Genesis 4:9), the Hebrew word for 'know' has a wide range of meaning, including sexual relations (Genesis 4:1). Here the term denotes God's sovereign choice, or election, of Israel as the object of His loving concern (Genesis 18:19; compare Deuteronomy 7:7-8)."[1]

3. What is the special significance of the statements in 3:7-8?

_____

_____

_____

_____

The Sovereign LORD does nothing without revealing his plan to his servants the prophets (3:7). "Amos's faith, which was based on his intimacy with God, may be difficult for us to comprehend, but God desires a similar intimacy of faith from all his people (Jeremiah 31:33-34; John 14:21)."[2]

4. Summarize God's message of judgment in 3:9-11.

_____

_____

_____

_____

Enemy (3:11). Assyria.

76

5. What punishment does God promise Israel in 3:12-15?

_____

_____

_____

_____

6. Summarize God's message and its significance in Amos 4:1-3.

_____

_____

_____

_____

Cows of Bashan (4:1). "Upper-class women, directly addressed, are compared with the best breed of cattle in ancient Canaan, which were raised (and pampered) in the pastures of northern Transjordan."[3] "This use of irony is especially stinging because it is addressed to women of wealth and stature, who may have secretly felt that they deserved to be addressed in a style accorded to gods and royalty."[4]

7. What is the emphasis of God's sarcastic message in 4:4-5?

_____

_____

_____

8. a. Summarize the situation that God describes in 4:6-11 and what this reveals about His heart and character.

_____

Optional Application: Review again the hardheartedness and rebelliousness of the people as portrayed in 4:6-11. In what ways does this passage reflect the tendencies of your own heart and point to your continuing need to experience the grace that's found in the gospel of Jesus Christ?

For Further Study: Reflect again on the truths about God set forth in Amos 4:13. Explore the links with these truths you see in the following New Testament passages: Matthew 9:4; John 1:5,9; 2:25; 3:8; Ephesians 2:6; Hebrews 4:12.

Optional Application: The powerful words to Israel ring out in Amos 4:12: "Prepare to meet your God." What does it mean for *you* to be prepared to meet God?

b. The refrain here repeats, "Yet you have not returned to me" (4:6,8,9,10,11). Explain why the people stubbornly resisted the Lord in spite of the severe discipline He sent their way?

_____

_____

_____

_____

9. a. What is the special significance of the Lord's pronouncements in 4:12-13?

_____

_____

_____

_____

b. What attributes of God are highlighted most in the words of 4:13?

_____

_____

_____

_____

10. Summarize the message for Israel recorded in Amos 5:1-3.

_____

_____

_____

_____

11. What is the Lord asking the people essentially to do in 5:4-6?

_____

_____

_____

_____

Seek me and live (5:4). "The Lord had promised to meet those who would seek Him, even in exile (Deuteronomy 4:29; compare Lamentations 3:25). Tragically, the Lord's people often did not seek Him (Isaiah 9:13; Jeremiah 10:21)."[5]

---

12. What are we meant to learn most about God from His words in 5:8-9?

_____

_____

_____

_____

13. What fault is the Lord finding with His people in 5:10-13?

_____

_____

_____

_____

The prudent keep quiet (5:13). "He knows he cannot change the state of affairs, and therefore only awaits judgment."[6] "The times will be so bad that the truth will not be tolerated."[7] "As a nation deepens in sin, wisdom becomes increasingly rare."[8]

Optional Application: Again, the Lord's powerful words ring out: "Seek me and live. . . . Seek the LORD and live" (Amos 5:4,6). At this time in your life, what does it mean most for *you* to seek the Lord? And what does it mean to really *live*?

Optional Application: Reflect again on the truths about God that are taught in Amos 5:8-9. What importance and relevance do these truths have in your own understanding and worship of God?

For Further Study:
How does the obser-
vation made in Amos
5:13 compare with
the prophetic words
spoken by Moses
in Deuteronomy
32:28-29?

**For Thought and
Discussion:** Review
the observation
made in Amos 5:13.
When is it accept-
able for a person to
remain quiet when
surrounded by evil?
When is it *not* right to
do so?

14. What is the Lord asking the people to do in
    5:14-15?

    _____

    _____

    _____

    _____

15. What is being portrayed in 5:16-17, and what is
    the significance of this?

    _____

    _____

    _____

    _____

16. What do we learn further about the "day of the
    Lord" in 5:18-20?

    _____

    _____

    _____

    _____

The day of the Lord (5:18,20). See also Amos
    8:9-10.

---

17. What do we learn about what God desires and
    expects from His people in 5:21-27?

    _____

    _____

    _____

    _____

18. Who are the words of Amos 6:1-7 directed to,
    and what is God's message to them?

_____

_____

_____

_____

For Further Study:
Reflect again on the
theme of "the day
of the LORD" in Amos
5:18-20. Compare
this with the proph-
ecies concerning
the "day of the
LORD" in these pas-
sages: Isaiah 2:12-21;
13:6-13; Jeremiah
46:10; Ezekiel 7:10-14;
Joel 1:15; 2:1,11,31;
3:14; Obadiah 15;
Zephaniah 1:7,14-16;
Malachi 4:5.

Kalneh . . . great Hamath . . . Gath in Philistia
(6:2). "Stronger cities than either Jerusalem or
Samaria had already fallen. Among these were
Calneh, in south-central Mesopotamia (see
Genesis 10:10; Isaiah 10:9); Hamath, in Syria to
the north of Israel; and Gath, a Philistine city
southeast of Israel. Since the three locations
reflect the entire extent of the so-called 'Fertile Crescent,' they may have been chosen for
their representative value. No city in the whole
region could claim immunity to destruction."[9]

19. What is the emphasis in God's message to His
people in 6:8-14?

_____

_____

_____

_____

**Optional
Application:** Reflect
again on God's words
in Amos 6:8. Is there
any "pride" in your
life, or are there any
"fortresses" in your
life, that God hates?
How can you answer
this question in a
humble, truthful, and
God-pleasing way?

***If ten people are left in one house, they too
will die*** (6:9). "While the general sense of this
vignette [6:9-11] is clear—nothing would be
left of the great houses and families—the
specific sense is not as clear. Perhaps it
describes a time when the survivors (verse 10)
would be so traumatized that they would be
afraid of any mention of the name of the Lord
lest it be done inappropriately and bring yet
more disaster upon them."[10]

Lo Debar (6:13). The name means "Nothing."
Karnaim (6:13). The name means "Horns"
(a symbol of strength). "Their names have a
special significance in this context. Israel is

rejoicing in what it has done through its own strength. This is a fatal attitude. It imagines substantial victory where there is, in fact, nothing. It fancies that it has horns of power, when in fact . . . they will gore nothing."[11]

From Lebo Hamath to the valley of the Arabah
(6:14). "The northern and southern boundaries of the kingdom as restored by Jeroboam II (2 Kings 14:25)."[12]

20. In Amos 3–6, what would you select as the key verse or passage—one that best captures or reflects the dynamics of what these chapters are all about?

_____

_____

_____

_____

21. What do these chapters in Amos communicate most to you about the heart and character of God?

_____

_____

_____

_____

22. List any lingering questions you have about Amos 3–6.

_____

_____

_____

_____

_____

_____

For the group

Consider focusing your discussion for lesson 7 especially on some of the following issues, themes, and concepts recognized as major overall themes in Amos. Which of these are dealt with in some way in chapters 3–6, and how are they further developed there?

- Moral and ethical responsibility of individuals and societies
- Sin
- God's judgment
- God's blessing, restoration, and salvation

Questions 20–22 in lesson 7 are among those that may stimulate your best and most helpful discussion.

Remember to look also at the "For Thought and Discussion" questions in the margins.

1. *New Geneva Study Bible* (Nashville: Thomas Nelson, 1995), at Amos 3:2.
2. Jeff Niehaus, "Amos," *The Minor Prophets*, ed. Thomas Edward McComiskey (Grand Rapids, MI: Baker, 2009), 316.
3. *NIV Study Bible* (Grand Rapids, MI: Zondervan, 1985), at Amos 4:1.
4. Niehaus, 325.
5. *New Geneva*, at Amos 5:4.
6. *NIV*, at Amos 5:13.
7. *New Geneva*, at Amos 5:13.
8. Niehaus, 421.
9. *ESV Study Bible* (Wheaton, IL: Crossway, 2008), at Amos 6:2.
10. *ESV*, at Amos 6:9-11.
11. Niehaus, 446.
12. *New Geneva*, at Amos 6:14.

Mar. 13

AMOS 7–9

Visions of Judgment

"The Lord gives Amos a vision of what may come. It is a judgment that is consistent with the Lord's covenantal warnings."[1]

1. In the vision recorded in Amos 7:1-3, what is Amos shown, how does he respond, and what does the Lord then do?

A swarm of locusts to strip the land after the kings share had been harvested

"The Lord shows Amos a second vision that is even more terrible than the first."[2]

2. Again in 7:4-6, what is Amos shown, how does he respond, and what does the Lord then do? *he showed him a great fire that devoured the land the Lord relents and it doesn't happen*

For Thought and Discussion: In what ways does the attitude of Amos in 7:1-6 reflect an appropriate humility before God?

For Further Study: How do the developments in Amos 7:1-6 compare with what Moses experienced with God in Exodus 32:12-14?

Optional Application: What personal encouragement do you find in the Lord's answers to the prayers of His prophet in Amos 7:1-6? How can this be a model for your own prayers?

3. In 7:6-9, what is Amos shown, and what explanation for it does the Lord give?

a plumb line, the Lord says he will destroy all the high places, sanctuaries will be ruined and a sword will be used against the house of Jeroboam

The Lord relented (7:3,6). "The Lord relented as a result of prayer on the part of the prophet."[3]

4. What is Amos accused of in 7:10-13?

raising a conspiracy against Israel, Jeroboam will die by the sword and Israel will go into exile

Amaziah the priest of Bethel (7:10). "A representative of the established religious leadership, who had the ear of the king, opposed the prophecies of Amos. His words, *Amos has conspired against you*, were a lie."[4]

Don't prophesy anymore (7:13). "The fact that God's message was unpopular (2:12) and that it provoked a strong reaction in official quarters (7:12-13) did not deter Amos from taking his stand (7:14-15) and prophesying (7:16-17)."[5]

5. How does Amos respond in 7:14-17?

that his wife will become a prostitute his sons and daughters will die by the sword and his land will divided up and he will die in a pagan country

I was neither a prophet nor the son of a prophet
(7:14). "The sovereign nature of his calling is of
great spiritual importance. Amos did not seek
to be a prophet by joining a prophetic school or
guild (7:14). God made him a prophet and gave
him his message."[6]

For Further Study:
Note the reference in
Amos 8:9 to the dark-
ness of the day of the
Lord. Explore how
this relates to what
you see in the follow-
ing passages: Isaiah
13:10; 24:23; 34:4; 50:3;
Ezekiel 32:7-8; Joel
2:10,31; Micah 3:6.

6. What is Amos shown, and what does he hear, in
the vision recorded in 8:1-4?

a basket of ripe fruit

7. What message is given to God's people in 8:5-8?

He will punish them for their acts of cheating
there will be earth quakes
and the earth will be dark during the
day and religious feast will be times of mourning

8. Describe the coming destruction of Israel as
prophesied in 8:9-14.

the sun will go down at noon and the earth will
be dark

A famine of hearing the words of the Lord (8:11).
"In times of great distress Israel turned to the
Lord for a prophetic word of hope or guidance
(see, for example, 2 Kings 19:1-4,14; 22:13-14;
Jeremiah 21:2; Ezekiel 14:3,7), but in the com-
ing judgment the Lord will answer all such
appeals with silence—the awful silence of
God."[7]

For Further Study:
Reflect on the "fam-
ine of hearing the
words of the LORD"
foretold in Amos
8:11. Describe what
connections with
this you see in the
following passages:
Deuteronomy 32:20;
1 Samuel 3:1; 28:6;
Ezekiel 7:26; 20:1-3;
Micah 3:4,7.

**Optional
Application:** Reflect
again on the truths
about God that are
taught in Amos 9:5-6.
What importance and
relevance do these
truths have in your
own understanding
and worship of God?

**For Thought and
Discussion:** In Amos
9:1-10, we see the
Lord emphasizing
that His judgment is
inescapable. Is such
a message needed in
our culture today?

The sin of Samaria (8:14). "Presumably its Ash-
erah worship."[8]

9. In Amos 9:1-4, what does the prophet see and
hear?

*the Lord stand by the alter
saying stike the top of the pillar
bringing them down on the people
they will not be able to hide from
God's wrath*

10. What is emphasized about the Lord in the prophetic words of 9:5-6?

*the power of the Lord in
all things*

11. What is emphasized in the Lord's words to His
people Israel in 9:7-10?

*What the Lord had done
for the Israelites and how
he help the other nations
as well
God takes care of his people*

Cushites (9:7). "Cushites (or Nubians), who lived
south of Egypt, were considered to be living
at the end of the world. All peoples are under
God's providential care."[9]

Caphtor (9:7). Crete.

12. Summarize the promises that are given to
God's people in 9:11-15 and their significance.

Restore David fallen tent

repair the broken places and ruins

In Amos 9:13 we see "a beautiful poetic image of a land like the garden of Eden — with productivity that is free from the curse (Genesis 3:17-19; compare Amos 4:6-10) and with greater abundance than anything currently known."[10]

13. In Amos 7–9, what would you select as the key verse or passage — one that best captures or reflects the dynamics of what these chapters are all about?

V8   Surely the eyes of the sovereign Lord are on the sinful nation, I will destroy it but not totally only the sinners

14. What do these chapters in Amos communicate most to you about the heart and character of God?

God loves his people like a parent loves a child, he will punish but not destroy but only to bring about obedience

15. List any lingering questions you have about Amos 7–9.

Reviewing the book of Amos

16. In your study of the book of Amos, what have you learned and appreciated most?

_____

_____

_____

_____

17. From this book, what are your overall impressions of the character and personality of the prophet Amos?

_____

_____

_____

_____

18. Recall the message of Isaiah 55:10-11 — in the same way God sends rain and snow from the sky to water the earth and nurture life, so also He sends His words to accomplish specific purposes. What would you suggest are God's primary purposes for the message of Amos in the lives of His people today?

_____

_____

_____

_____

19. Review the guidelines in Philippians 4:8 — "Whatever is true, whatever is noble, whatever is right, whatever is pure, whatever is lovely, whatever is admirable — if anything is excellent or praiseworthy — *think about such things*" (emphasis added). As you reflect on all you've read in this book of Amos, what stands out to you as being particularly *true*, or *noble*, or *right*, or *pure*, or *lovely*, or *admirable*, or *excellent*, or

praiseworthy—and therefore well worth thinking more about?

_____

_____

_____

_____

Optional Application: Which verses in Amos would be most helpful for you to memorize so you have them always available in your mind and heart for the Holy Spirit to use?

20. Considering that all of Scripture testifies ultimately of Christ, where does Jesus come most in focus for you in this book?

_____

_____

_____

_____

21. In your understanding, what are the strongest ways in which Amos points us to mankind's need for Jesus and for what He accomplished in His death and resurrection?

_____

_____

_____

_____

22. Recall Paul's reminder in Romans 15:4 that the Old Testament Scriptures can give us patience and perseverance as well as comfort and encouragement. In your own life, how do you see the book of Amos living up to Paul's description? In what ways do the Old Testament Scriptures help meet your personal need for both perseverance and encouragement?

_____

_____

_____

_____

For the group

Consider focusing your discussion for lesson 8 especially on some of the following issues, themes, and concepts recognized as major overall themes in Amos. Which of these are dealt with in some way in chapters 7–9, and how are they further developed there?

- Moral and ethical responsibility of individuals and societies
- Sin
- God's judgment
- God's blessing, restoration, and salvation

Questions 15–22 in lesson 8 are among those that may stimulate your best and most helpful discussion.

Once more, look also at the questions in the margins under the heading "For Thought and Discussion."

1. Jeff Niehaus, "Amos," *The Minor Prophets*, ed. Thomas Edward McComiskey (Grand Rapids, MI: Baker, 2009), 450–451.
2. Niehaus, 454.
3. Niehaus, 452.
4. *ESV Study Bible* (Wheaton, IL: Crossway, 2008), at Amos 7:10.
5. Niehaus, 316.
6. Niehaus, 316.
7. *NIV Study Bible* (Grand Rapids, MI: Zondervan, 1985), at Amos 8:11.
8. Niehaus, 476.
9. *ESV Study Bible*, at Amos 9:7.
10. *ESV*, at Amos 9:13.

OBADIAH

A Nation Judged for Mistreating God's People

Obadiah is the Old Testament's shortest book. "It is unique among Old Testament prophetic books in being directed against a foreign nation, without any oracles of judgment against either Israel or Judah."[1]

"The prophet has in view a military assault on Jerusalem in which the Edomites gleefully took part (verses 11-14), but he does not provide information that clearly dates the catastrophe. Some date the book in relation to an invasion of Judah by Philistines and Arabs during King Jehoram's reign (848–841 B.C.), in which it is presumed that the Edomites participated (2 Kings 8:20-22; 2 Chronicles 21:8-10,16,17). Others relate the events prompting this prophecy to the invasion of Judah by the Babylonians, which resulted eventually in her collapse in 586 B.C. Both Scripture (Psalm 137; Ezekiel 35:1-15) and Jewish tradition explicitly mention the Edomites' involvement in this final catastrophe, and the text of Obadiah seems to refer more naturally to this event."[2]

"The prophecy is 'concerning Edom' (verse 1) and is repeatedly addressed to that nation, but it was given to the covenant community as holy Scripture. The purpose, therefore, more than to warn Edom of imminent judgment, is to reassure God's people of His triumphant justice at work for them. . . .

"When the church suffers at the hands of God's enemies, she needs to return to the prophecy of Obadiah and renew her faith in the just God revealed there. He cares for His persecuted people, and behind their present circumstances He is always at work for them."[3]

1. In Jeremiah 23:29, God says that His Word is "like fire" and "like a hammer." He can use the Scriptures to burn away unclean thoughts and desires in our hearts. He can also use Scripture, with hammer-like hardness, to crush and crumble our spiritual hardness. From your study of Obadiah, how do you most want to see the fire-and-hammer power of God's Word at work in your life? Express this longing in a written prayer to God.

_____

_____

_____

_____

2. How does verse 1 set the stage for this book?

It came from a vision
of Obadiah

Edom (verse 1). "The Edomites were descendants of Esau, so that the hostility between them and the Israelites goes back ultimately to the sibling rivalry of Jacob and Esau; when the Israelites were devastated by foreign armies, the Edomites did not feel any sympathy toward the Israelites because of their blood ties but instead gloated over their defeat and looted them."[4]

An envoy was sent to the nations (verse 1). "The judgment scene that Obadiah describes is the sphere of the nations. A spiritual envoy from Yahweh enters the arena of national affairs to bring judgment on Edom. This act of Yahweh portends judgment on all nations that commit gross evil."[5]

3. Summarize how Obadiah depicts the destruction of Edom in verses 1-9.

God will destroy Edom
because their allies will
desert them, or overpower them
because of Edom deceit

"Accounts such as this . . . remind us that our Lord will act on behalf of those who belong to him. This is why we are commanded, 'Be strong in the Lord and in the strength of his power' (Ephesians 6:10). Only his power, in and through us,

Optional Application: We read that after Jesus' resurrection, when He was explaining Old Testament passages to His disciples, He "opened their minds so they could understand the Scriptures" (Luke 24:45). Ask God to do that kind of work in *your* mind as you study the book of Obadiah so you're released and free to learn everything here He wants you to learn and so you can become as bold, worshipful, and faithful as those early disciples of Jesus. Express this desire to Him in prayer.

For Thought and Discussion: How familiar is the book of Obadiah to you? What have been your previous impressions of this book?

For Further Study:
What similarities do you see between the first nine verses of Obadiah and Jeremiah 49:7-22?

For Further Study:
What additional record do you see of God's judgment against Edom in Psalm 108:9, Isaiah 34:5-15, Ezekiel 25:15-17, Amos 1:11-12, and Malachi 1:2-5?

makes the warfare of God's kingdom successful." [6]

"Edom's hostile activities have spanned the centuries of Israel's existence. The following Biblical references are helpful in understanding the relation of Israel and Edom: Genesis 27:41-45; 32:1-21; 33; 36; Exodus 15:15; Numbers 20:14-21; Deuteronomy 2:1-6; 23:7; 1 Samuel 21 with Psalm 52; 2 Samuel 8:13-14; 2 Kings 8:20-22; 14:7; Psalm 83; Ezekiel 35; Joel 3:18-19; Amos 1:11-12; 9:12." [7]

4. What faults and weaknesses on the part of Edom does this passage emphasize?

   violence to Jacob
   _____
   _____
   _____

5. What particular sins of Edom are emphasized in verses 10-14, and why do you think these particular ones are singled out?

   violence to Jacob
   did nothing to help
   _____
   _____
   _____

Violence against your brother Jacob (1:10).
"Since the Edomites are related to the Israelites, their hostility is all the more reprehensible." [8]

96

6. Summarize God's warning and promise toward all nations in verses 15-16.

will suffer as they
made other suffer

For Further Study: Compare and review what you see in verse 15 with prophecies concerning the "day of the LORD" in these passages: Isaiah 2:12-21; 13:6-13; Jeremiah 46:10; Ezekiel 7:10-14; Joel 1:15; 2:1,11,31; 3:14; Amos 5:18-20; 8:9-10; Zephaniah 1:7,14-16; Malachi 4:5.

Optional Application: We read in Obadiah 15, "The day of the LORD is near for all nations." What does this nearness mean personally for you?

As you have done, it will be done to you; your deeds will return upon your own head (1:15). "The same standard of justice applies throughout history, on the individual level as well as the international. So Jesus declares: 'Do not judge, so that you may not be judged. For with the judgment you make you will be judged, and the measure you give will be the measure you get' (Matthew 7:1-2). The apostle Paul affirms the same concept in Romans 2:1-11. Knowing this, let us not live as Edomites—as those hostile to God and as those who have no hope (1 Thessalonians 4:13). But let God's people live out Christ Jesus—who is in us, the hope of glory."[9]

7. State in your own words the thrust and emphasis of the promises toward God's people as given in verses 17-21.

Nations will fail
and

Mount Zion (verse 17). "The place where Yahweh dwelt among and for his people. Those gathered around his presence and taking refuge in him will be delivered from the coming wrath (Isaiah 14:32). In principle, Zion's blessings were available to Gentiles (1 Kings 8:41-43; Isaiah 2:2-4)."[10]

For Further Study:
How does the truth about Mount Zion in Obadiah 17 compare with what you see in Hebrews 12:22-24?

For Further Study:
In verse 18, we see a stark contrast between "Jacob" and "Esau." Look further at Genesis 25:23, Malachi 1:3, and Romans 9:13. What do these passages emphasize for our better understanding of the relationship between the descendants of Jacob and Esau?

For Further Study:
Compare the message of Obadiah 21 with what you see in the words of Jesus in Matthew 19:28 and the words of Paul in 1 Corinthians 6:2-3. What links do you see?

8. What special significance do you see in God's promises in verse 21?

_____

_____

Kingdom will be the

Lord

_____

Deliverers (verse 21). "Those appointed by God to deliver the people and bring just governance."[11] "God's people, transformed from fugitives (verse 14) into deliverers, will reign over what was once enemy-held territory."[12]

Mount Zion (verse 21). Compare Isaiah 2:1-5. _____

9. In the rich and striking imagery that marks Obadiah's words in this book, which images stand out most strongly to you and why?

We will be Judged by

what we do

_____

_____

10. What have you learned or appreciated most in your study of the book of Obadiah?

_____

_____

_____

_____

11. In the book of Obadiah, what would you select as the key verse or passage—one that best captures or reflects the dynamics of what this book is all about?

_____

_√ 2/_

12. What does the book of Obadiah communicate most to you about the heart and character of God?

13. List any lingering questions you have about the book of Obadiah.

14. Recall the message of Isaiah 55:10-11 — in the same way God sends rain and snow from the sky to water the earth and nurture life, so also He sends His words to accomplish specific purposes. What would you suggest are God's primary purposes for the message of Obadiah in the lives of His people today?

15. Review Philippians 4:8 — "Whatever is true, whatever is noble, whatever is right, whatever is pure, whatever is lovely, whatever is admirable — if anything is excellent or praiseworthy — *think about such things*" (emphasis

99

Optional Application: Which verse or verses in the book of Obadiah would be most helpful for you to memorize so you have them always available in your mind and heart for the Holy Spirit to use?

added). As you reflect on all you've read in this book of Obadiah, what stands out to you as being particularly *true*, or *noble*, or *right*, or *pure*, or *lovely*, or *admirable*, or *excellent*, or *praiseworthy* — and therefore well worth thinking more about?

_____

_____

_____

_____

16. Considering that all of Scripture testifies ultimately of Christ, where does *Jesus* come most in focus for you in this book?

_____

_____

_____

_____

17. In your understanding, what are the strongest ways in which Obadiah points us to mankind's need for Jesus and for what He accomplished in His death and resurrection?

_____

_____

_____

_____

18. Recall Paul's reminder in Romans 15:4 that the Old Testament Scriptures can give us patience and perseverance as well as comfort and encouragement. In your own life, how do you see the book of Obadiah living up to Paul's description? In what ways do the Old Testament Scriptures help meet your personal need for both perseverance and encouragement?

_____

_____

_____

_____

For the group

Consider focusing your discussion for lesson 9 especially on the following issues, themes, and concepts
recognized as major overall themes in Obadiah.
How do you see these being dealt with in this book?

- Judgment from God
- Deliverance from God
- Blessing from God
- God's sovereignty
- God's justice
- God's mercy

    Questions 12–18 in lesson 9 are among those
that may stimulate your best and most helpful
discussion.
    Look also at the question in the margin under
the heading "For Thought and Discussion."

1. Leland Ryken and Philip Graham Ryken, eds., introduction
   to Obadiah, "The Book at a Glance," *The Literary Study
   Bible* (Wheaton, IL: Crossway, 2007).
2. *New Geneva Study Bible*, introduction to Obadiah, "Date
   and Occasion," (Nashville: Thomas Nelson, 1995).
3. *New Geneva*, introduction to Obadiah, "Characteristics and
   Themes."
4. Ryken and Ryken, *Literary Study Bible*, Introduction to
   Obadiah, "Historical backdrop."
5. Jeff Niehaus, "Obadiah," *The Minor Prophets*, ed. Thomas
   Edward McComiskey (Grand Rapids, MI: Baker, 2009), 513.
6. Niehaus, 525.
7. *NIV*, introduction to Obadiah, "Unity and Theme" (Grand
   Rapids, MI: Zondervan, 1985).
8. *NIV*, introduction to Obadiah, "Unity and Theme."
9. Niehaus, 535.
10. *ESV Study Bible* (Wheaton, IL: Crossway, 2008), at Obadiah
    17.
11. *ESV*, at Obadiah 21.
12. *New Geneva*, at Obadiah 21.

JONAH

God's Unimaginable Grace and Mercy

"The story of Jonah is one of the best-known stories in the Bible. The book that tells this story is a missionary manual on the subject of the universal (as opposed to single-group) scope of God's salvation."[1]

"Some have called the Book of Jonah the 'Acts of the Old Testament' because it graphically demonstrates that God is willing to have mercy on all who seek Him in humility and sincerity. The repentance of the people of Nineveh postponed the destruction of their city for roughly 150 years (until 612 B.C.)."[2]

"The great merit of the book is that it comments objectively on the human scene, especially the religious side of it, from the divine viewpoint. Here lies the secret of the book's continuing story. What one makes of it will depend partly

Optional Application: We read that after Jesus' resurrection, when He was explaining Old Testament passages to His disciples, He "opened their minds so they could understand the Scriptures" (Luke 24:45). Ask God to do that kind of work in your mind as you study the book of Jonah so you're released and free to learn everything here He wants you to learn and so you can become as bold, worshipful, and faithful as those early disciples of Jesus. Express this desire to Him in prayer.

For Thought and Discussion: What have been your past impressions of Jonah's story?

For Further Study: How do the words of Jesus in Matthew 12:40-41 and Luke 11:32 confirm the historical accuracy of the book of Jonah?

on self-understanding and partly on one's grasp of the all-embracing love of the God we serve."[3]

1. In Jeremiah 23:29, God says that His Word is "like fire" and "like a hammer." He can use the Scriptures to burn away unclean thoughts and desires in our hearts. He can also use Scripture, with hammer-like hardness, to crush and crumble our spiritual hardness. From your study of Jonah, how do you most want to see the fire-and-hammer power of God's Word at work in your life? Express this longing in a written prayer to God.

_____

_____

_____

_____

2. What did God call this man to do, according to Jonah 1:1-2?

Preach against the people of Ninevah

_____

_____

Wickedness (1:2). "The same Hebrew word can mean *evil* or *disaster*, depending on the context."[4] This key word is found a total of nine times in Jonah and translated variously: "Who is responsible for this calamity" (1:7); "Who is responsible for making all this *trouble* for us?" (1:8, emphasis added); "Let them give up their *evil* ways" (3:8, emphasis added); "When God saw . . . how they turned from their evil ways, he relented and did not bring on them the *destruction* he had threatened" (3:10, emphasis added); "to Jonah this seemed very wrong" (4:1); "I knew that you are . . . a God who relents from sending calamity" (4:2); "the LORD God provided a leafy plant . . . to ease his *discomfort*" (4:6, emphasis added).

Tarshish (1:3). "Perhaps the city of Tartessus in southwest Spain, a Phoenician mining colony near Gibraltar. By heading in the opposite direction from Nineveh, to what seemed like the end of the world, Jonah intended to escape his divinely appointed task."[5]

For Further Study: What previous ministry on the part of the prophet Jonah (during the reign of Israel's King Amaziah) do we read about in 2 Kings 14:23-27? What does this reveal about the man Jonah?

3. According to 1:3, how did Jonah respond?

he fled from the hard by boarding a ship to Tarshish

4. Describe the significance of what happens next (see verses 4-6).

the sailors recognized that Jonah could talk to God and ask your God for relief from the storm they recognized the power of Jonah's God

5. Summarize the events of 1:7-10 and what they reveal about Jonah and the others on the ship.

1) the sailors believed someone was responsible for the weather 2) Jonah believed in God the others didn't. 3) they believed Jonah was responsible for their plite

I worship the LORD (1:9). "His actions contradict his confession."[6]

6. a. Summarize the further developments that lead to Jonah's being thrown overboard.

the sailors believed that Jonah was the cause of their situation. Jonah suggested that they throw him over board to save themselves

b. What do these verses further reveal about Jonah and the others on the ship?

Jonah trusted the Lord the others finally came to God and asked for forgiveness for what they were about to do.

c. How do the other sailors indicate here their faith in the Lord?

they asked for forgiveness for throwing Jonah overboard.

Fish (1:17). "A general word for an aquatic beast, which cannot be identified further. However, a large whale such as a sperm whale could easily swallow a man whole."[7]

---

7. In the way 1:17 is worded, what aspects of this statement seem especially significant?

God provided a means for Jonah to be saved.

8. a. In Jonah's prayer (see 2:1-9), what else do we learn about his physical surroundings and what has happened to him?

Jonah recognized that salvation comes from the Lord and this saved him

Jesus in heart of earth

b. According to these same verses, what is happening in Jonah's heart and soul?

Jonah recognized that only God could save him. and he prayed for God help in his time of need - God answered him with salvation

Shouts of grateful praise (2:9). "Jonah's response to God's judgment is framed in the form of a thanksgiving psalm. The cry of the prophet focuses on the desperate character of his situation by using terms typical in poetic descriptions of death or nearness to death. In his plight he looks to the Lord's holy temple, the physical token of the Lord's saving presence with His people. The psalm is a moving testimony to the heart of Israel's faith and to the heart of the prophet, but he still had much to learn. His vision of God's mercy was still narrow."[9]

9. In the way that 2:10 is worded, what aspects of this statement seem especially significant?

God has commanded all things

10. In 3:1-2, what does the Lord call Jonah to do, and how does this relate to his first calling in 1:1-2?

God commands Jonah to give a message to the city of Nineveh

second chance city of

Three days (3:3). "The phrase may refer to the time it would take Jonah to walk throughout the city, preaching the message. ('Nineveh' could also refer to the much larger administrative area including the city and the outlying villages, which was 30–56 miles across.)"[10]

11. What is especially significant about Jonah's response in 3:3-4?

Jonah obeys God and goes to Nineveh and tells them of the coming disaster

12. Summarize the response of the ruler and people of Nineveh as described in 3:5-9.

they believed Jonahs message from God and when the king gave the command that everyone call on God and repent of their evil

ways and violence God had compassion and did not destroy them

King (3:6). "Apparently a reference to the mighty king of Assyria."[11]

And animals (3:8). "Inclusion of the domestic animals was unusual and expressed the urgency with which the Ninevites sought mercy."[12]

13. What is especially significant in the Lord's response to the Ninevites in 3:10?

His compassion when he saw the people turning from their evil ways

Although the people of Nineveh repented after hearing from Jonah the pronouncement of God's coming wrath (see Jonah 3:5-10), and God then withheld His judgment, later generations would not follow their example. Nineveh returned to wickedness, as we see emphasized in the book of the prophet Nahum. And eventually (before the end of the seventh century BC), Nineveh would indeed be destroyed under God's hand of judgment.

14. What are the most revealing aspects in Jonah's response to this situation, as seen in 4:1-3?

He prayed to God and asked him to take his life but God asked if he (Jonah) had any right to be angry

To Jonah this seemed very wrong (4:1). "The Hebrew is particularly vivid (literally 'it was evil to Jonah as a great wrong')."[13]

Take away my life (4:3). "Jonah shortly before had rejoiced in his deliverance from death, but now that Nineveh lives, he prefers to die."[14]

109

For Further Study:
For background to Jonah's words about God's loving character in Jonah 4:2, see God's words to Moses in Exodus 34:6. (See also Psalm 86:5,15; 103:8; 145:8.)

15. What significance do you see in the Lord's question to Jonah in 4:4?

God is asking Jonah to examine his anger to see if it is justified.

16. Summarize the things that happen in Jonah's story in 4:5-8 and the significance of these things.

God uses this example of first providing and then taking away because Jonah did not take care of what God had provided.

Jonah had gone out. . . . He made himself a shelter (4:5). "Hoping that the Lord will execute judgment, Jonah leaves the city for a vantage point from which to view the destruction of the city."[15]

"The divine intention of the object lessons is now revealed. God's magnificent compassion for the people and animals He created and sustained (4:11) is contrasted with Jonah's petty concern for the plant (4:10). The reader recalls the compassion of Jesus as He looked upon the multitudes (Matthew 9:36; Mark 6:34; 8:2), and His statement in Matthew 10:29 that not a sparrow will fall to the ground apart from the will of the Father. In its infancy, the largely Jewish New Testament church would again wrestle

110

with this issue of the wideness of God's mercy, as the Lord opened the hearts of the Gentiles to obey the gospel (Acts 11:18; 15:14; 28:28)."[16]

For Thought and Discussion: From your perspective, what was at the root of Jonah's wrong reactions as described in chapter 4? What did he fail to understand about himself, other people, and God?

Optional Application: To what extent can you relate personally to Jonah's reactions in chapter 4? Do you share, in any way, some of the wrong assumptions Jonah was clinging to?

17. How would you explain the Lord's question to Jonah—and Jonah's answer—in 4:9?

self-righteous anger

Jonah did nothing to make the vine grow and had no claim to it so he should not have expected it it continue to provide comfort

18. What is the Lord saying about Jonah in 4:10? Describe this in your own words.

Jonah was taking a lot for granted without recognizing how God was helping him

19. What significance do you see in the Lord's question to Jonah in the final verse of this book (see 4:11)?

We need to be concerned about more than ourselves

"The question with which the book ends highlights the contrast between the Lord's love for the pagan city, and Jonah's anger that it should have been forgiven. The tension is left unresolved."[17]

Cannot tell their right hand from their left
(4:11). "An idiom for being morally and spiritually unaware, that probably refers to the entire population."[18]

And also many animals (4:11). "The ironic question raised by these words is: If Jonah will not allow God to have compassion on Nineveh for the sake of the 120,000 people whom God created and cares for, will Jonah not allow God to have compassion on Nineveh for the sake of the animals, since after all, Jonah was willing to have compassion on a plant? The question is left unanswered so that the readers of the book may answer it for themselves."[19]

20. In your study of Jonah's story, what have you learned and appreciated most?

_____

_____

_____

_____

21. In this book of Jonah, what would you select as the key verse or passage—one that best captures or reflects the dynamics of what this book is all about?

_____

_____

_____

_____

22. What does the book of Jonah communicate most to you about the heart and character of God?

_____

_____

_____

_____

23. List any lingering questions you have about the book of Jonah.

_____

_____

_____

_____

24. Recall the message of Isaiah 55:10-11 — in the same way God sends rain and snow from the sky to water the earth and nurture life, so also He sends His words to accomplish specific purposes. What would you suggest are God's primary purposes for the message of Jonah in the lives of His people today?

_____

_____

_____

_____

25. Review Philippians 4:8 — "Whatever is true, whatever is noble, whatever is right, whatever is pure, whatever is lovely, whatever is admirable—if anything is excellent or praiseworthy — *think about such things*" (emphasis added). As you reflect on all you've read in this book of Jonah, what stands out to you as being particularly *true*, or *noble*, or *right*, or *pure*, or *lovely*, or *admirable*, or *excellent*, or *praiseworthy* — and therefore well worth thinking more about?

_____

_____

_____

_____

26. Considering that all of Scripture testifies ultimately of Christ, where does Jesus come most in focus for you in this book?

_____

Optional Application: Which verse or verses in the book of Jonah would be most helpful for you to memorize so you have them always available in your mind and heart for the Holy Spirit to use?

_____

_____

_____

_____

27. In your understanding, what are the strongest ways in which Jonah points us to mankind's need for Jesus and for what He accomplished in His death and resurrection?

_____

_____

_____

_____

28. Recall Paul's reminder in Romans 15:4 that the Old Testament Scriptures can give us patience and perseverance as well as comfort and encouragement. In your own life, how do you see the book of Jonah living up to Paul's description? In what ways do the Old Testament Scriptures help meet your personal need for both perseverance and encouragement?

_____

_____

_____

_____

For the group

Consider focusing your discussion for lesson 10 especially on the following issues, themes, and concepts recognized as major overall themes in Jonah. How do you see these being dealt with in this book?

- God's calling
- God's guidance
- God's mercy and saving love for all people of all nations
- God's mercy to His servants

- Repentance
- Faith
- Bigotry and ethnocentrism
- Obedience to God's guidance and calling

Questions 21–28 in lesson 10 are among those that may stimulate your best and most helpful discussion.

Look also at the questions in the margins under the heading "For Thought and Discussion."

1. Leland Ryken and Philip Graham Ryken, eds., introduction to Jonah, "The Book at a Glance," *The Literary Study Bible* (Wheaton, IL: Crossway, 2007).
2. Warren Baker, ed., *The Complete Word Study Old Testament* (Chattanooga, TN: AMG Publishers, 1994), introduction to Jonah.
3. Joyce Baldwin, "Jonah," *The Minor Prophets*, ed. Thomas Edward McComiskey (Grand Rapids, MI: Baker, 2009), 548.
4. *ESV Study Bible* (Wheaton, IL: Crossway, 2008), at Jonah 1:2.
5. *NIV Study Bible* (Grand Rapids, MI: Zondervan, 1985), at Jonah 1:3.
6. *ESV,* at Jonah 1:9-10.
7. *ESV,* at Jonah 1:17.
8. Ryken and Ryken, *Literary Study Bible*, introduction to Jonah, "The book of Jonah as a chapter in the master story of the Bible."
9. *New Geneva Study Bible* (Nashville: Thomas Nelson, 1995), at Jonah 2:1-10.
10. *ESV,* at Jonah 3:3.
11. *New Geneva,* at Jonah 3:6.
12. *NIV,* at Jonah 3:8.
13. *New Geneva,* at Jonah 4:1.
14. *NIV,* at Jonah 4:3.
15. *New Geneva,* at Jonah 4:5.
16. *New Geneva,* at Jonah 4:9-11.
17. Baldwin, 543.
18. *ESV,* at Jonah 4:10-11.
19. *ESV,* at Jonah 4:10-11.

MICAH 1–4

Judgment upon the Nations

"Both Micah and his contemporary Isaiah ministered in the Southern Kingdom (Judah). Micah's ministry, however, began somewhat later than Isaiah's and may have ended earlier. Their social standings were quite different in that Isaiah was a nobleman who prophesied in the king's court and Micah was of humble origin and spoke to the common people. Nevertheless, the prophecies of both were of great importance."[1]

"The main subject of the prophetic book of Micah is how God deals with sinful humanity.... The implied purpose of Micah the prophet is to warn all people, especially God's people, that God does not tolerate sin and, along with that, to instill an attitude of repentance. Micah assumes that the information that the human race most needs is a double message—the bad news that the

Optional Application: We read that after Jesus' resurrection, when He was explaining Old Testament passages to His disciples, He "opened their minds so they could understand the Scriptures" (Luke 24:45). Ask God to do that kind of work in *your* mind as you study the book of Micah so you're released and free to learn everything here He wants you to learn and so you can become as bold, worshipful, and faithful as those early disciples of Jesus. Express this desire to Him in prayer.

For Thought and Discussion: How familiar is the book of Micah to you? What have been your previous impressions of this book?

For Further Study: For more background on the kings mentioned in Micah 1:1, see 2 Kings 15:32-38 and 2 Chronicles 27:1-9 (for Jotham), 2 Kings 16 and 2 Chronicles 28 (for Ahaz), and 2 Kings 18–20 and 2 Chronicles 29–32 (for Hezekiah).

human race is headed for disaster if left to its own inclinations and the good news that God offers salvation."[2]

1. In Jeremiah 23:29, God says that His Word is "like fire" and "like a hammer." He can use the Scriptures to burn away unclean thoughts and desires in our hearts. He can also use Scripture, with hammer-like hardness, to crush and crumble our spiritual hardness. From your study of Micah, how do you most want to see the fire-and-hammer power of God's Word at work in your life? Express this longing in a written prayer to God.

_____

_____

_____

_____

2. What do you know already about the kings mentioned in Micah 1:1?

Kings of Judah between
750 - 686 b.c.

_____

_____

Hear (1:2). This is "the key word in Micah. . . . God wanted Judah to be attentive to Micah's message."[3] See also 3:1,9; 6:1,2,9.

---

3. What does the Lord promise to do in Micah 1:2-7, and for what reasons?

God will turn against
Israel because of idol
worship

118

4. How would you summarize Micah's response to this (see 1:8-9)?

weepand whale
Intense mourning, go naked
he will howl like a jackal
moan like an owl

For Thought and Discussion: Micah 1:2 introduces a message for all the earth's peoples. Do the world's nations today need this message as well? If so, why? And will they be open to it?

Naked (1:8). "Clothed only in a loincloth."[4]

Plague (1:9). The word "signifies the slaughter and waste of the entire land through the onslaught of war (1 Kings 20:21)."[5]

5. Summarize the future for Judah that is prophesied in 1:10-17.

Israel will go into exile — they should shave their heads in mourning

"Using the names of towns taken by the Assyrians, Micah's extensive wordplay (in 1:10-15) reflects the various disasters that Judah will face."[6]

Tell it not in Gath (1:10). "Micah did not want the pagan people in Gath to gloat over the downfall of God's people."[7]

Beth Ophrah (1:10). Meaning "House of Dust."

Shaphir (1:11). The word "sounds like a related word for 'beautiful' and contrasts with 'nakedness and shame' [in verse 11]."[8]

119

Zaanan (1:11). Similar to the Hebrew word for "come out."

Beth Ezel (1:11). Meaning "House of Taking Away."

Maroth (1:12). Similar to the Hebrew word for "bitter."

Lachish (1:13). Similar to the Hebrew word for "team."

Moresheth Gath (1:14). Literally, "Possession of Gath."

Akzib (1:14). Meaning "Deception" or "Lie."

Mareshah (1:15). Literally, "Inheritance," or "Conquered."

Adullam (1:15). Literally, "Refuge."

6. In Micah 2:1-5, who are these prophecies directed toward, what wrongdoing do they expose, and what is their significance?

<u>those that hold themselves</u>
<u>to be better than others they</u>
<u>are wealthy and land owners</u>

"Until this prophecy the prophet spoke abstractly of rebellion and sin (Micah 1:5). Now he specifies the crime that has both social and theological dimensions."[9]

7. In Micah 2:6-11, who are these prophecies directed toward, what further accusations do they include, and what is their significance?

<u>the false prophets and those</u>
<u>who plan iniquities in</u>

order to acquire more
wealth

8. Summarize the essence of the picture given in Micah 2:12-13.

The Lord will lead his
people as he brings his
people to himself

"True prophets threatened judgment but promised salvation through it for the righteous remnant."[10]

Their King . . . the LORD (2:13). "The identity of the Shepherd-King who opened the breach and leads the people into battle is fully revealed."[11]

---

9. In Micah 3, who are these prophecies directed toward, and what is their significance?

the leaders of Israel, and those
who hate good and love evil to
those he predicts that darkness
will come over them and they will
no longer be able to prophise

10. What does Micah 3:8 reveal most about the prophet himself and his calling?

He believes and is filled with
power, the spirit and with
justice and might so they will
become a strong nation

For Thought and Discussion: In our world today, what forms of injustice are most in need of being exposed and combated?

Optional Application: What personal encouragement and hope do you find in the Lord's words in Micah 2:12-13 and what they reveal about Him and His plans for His people?

Optional Application: Think deeply about the words Micah expresses in Micah 3:8. To what extent do the same truths apply also to you, in your standing as a child of God the Father, redeemed by Jesus His Son, and indwelt and empowered by His Holy Spirit?

For Further Study: Note that Micah 4:1-3 is a parallel passage to Isaiah 2:1-4. Compare the context of both passages. What further connections and contrasts do you see?

those from exile those he has brought to grief and those who were driven away will be made a strong people

Filled with power, with the Spirit of the LORD (3:8). "The prophets were Spirit-filled messengers (see Isaiah 48:16)."[12]

"In a breathtaking turn, Micah shifts from the judicial sentence reducing Jerusalem into a heap of rubble and its temple into forested height to a vision of a future in which Jerusalem and its temple will become the center of global justice and righteousness and of international peace and prosperity."[13]

11. Summarize the most important details of God's promises as given in Micah 4:1-5.

   In the last days the kingdom of God will be established and God will teach the people his ways so they can walk on his paths

12. Summarize the most important details of God's promises as given in 4:6-8.

   In the last days God will restore his temple as chief in the mountains and people will stream to it, he will bring back the lame and

The LORD will rule over them in Mount Zion from that day and forever (4:7). "The prophecy now reaches its goal and climax.... Thus history will not repeat itself. The new and transformed nation will be ruled by God and his laws, not by debased leaders who rule according to their swollen appetites, as in the old."[14]

13. Summarize the future for Judah that is prophesied in 4:9-13.

*Judah will suffer by going
to Babylon, but will be rescued
by the Lord*

14. In Micah 1–4, what would you select as the key
verse or passage—one that best captures or
reflects the dynamics of what these chapters are
all about?

Micah 1: 2 – 16

15. What do these chapters in Micah communicate
most to you about the heart and character of
God?

*the Lord will prevail in his
plan*

16. List any lingering questions you have about
Micah 1–4.

For the group

Consider focusing your discussion for lesson 11 especially on some of the following issues, themes, and concepts recognized as major overall themes in Micah. Which of these are dealt with in some way in chapters 1–4, and how are they further developed there?

- God's judgment upon sin
- Salvation from God
- The sovereignty of God
- The future kingdom of God

Questions 14–16 in lesson 11 are among those that may stimulate your best and most helpful discussion.

Look also at the questions in the margins under the heading "For Thought and Discussion."

1. Warren Baker, ed., *The Complete Word Study Old Testament* (Chattanooga, TN: AMG Publishers, 1994), introduction to Micah.
2. Leland Ryken and Philip Graham Ryken, eds., introduction to Micah, "The Book at a Glance," *The Literary Study Bible* (Wheaton, IL: Crossway, 2007).
3. Baker, introduction to Micah.
4. *NIV Study Bible* (Grand Rapids, MI: Zondervan, 1985), at Micah 1:8.
5. Bruce K. Waltke, "Micah," *The Minor Prophets*, ed. Thomas Edward McComiskey (Grand Rapids, MI: Baker, 2009).
6. *ESV Study Bible* (Wheaton, IL: Crossway, 2008), at Micah 1:10-15.
7. *NIV*, at Micah 1:10.
8. *ESV*, at Micah 1:11.
9. Waltke, 635.
10. Waltke, 652.
11. *ESV*, at Micah 2:13.
12. *NIV*, at Micah 3:8.
13. Waltke, 676.
14. Waltke, 688.

MICAH 5–7

Leaders and People on Trial

1. Describe the new hope for Israel—and for the world—prophesied in Micah 5:1-6.

a new leader will come out of Bethlehem Ephrathah but until this leader comes Israel will be abandond

Bethlehem

Bethlehem Ephrathah (5:2). "The town of David's birth (1 Samuel 16:1-13). Though the Davidic line of kings would temporarily cease (Amos 5:3), God would yet raise up a ruler from David's family who would reign forever—Jesus Christ Himself (2 Samuel 7:12-17)."[1]

"Bethlehem . . . represents a new commencement, a new beginning, in the house of David. God will not frustrate his covenant with David but will gloriously fulfill it with a new David in the last days. Amazingly, God bypasses Jerusalem, the city he chose and loved above all cities (Psalms 46, 48, 76, 84, 87, 122), and in his

Optional Application:
What personal encouragement and comfort do you find in the description of Messiah — Jesus our Savior — in Micah 5:4-5?

For Thought and Discussion: The book of Micah speaks of a "remnant" of God's people (see 2:12; 4:7; 5:7-8; 7:18). How appropriate is it for the church today to think of itself as such?

divine election and enablement returns instead to the portal through which David stepped onto the stage of salvation-history when the Philistines threatened Israel with annihilation centuries before. Isaiah expressed the same truth of Messiah representing a new start by linking him with Jesse . . . (Isaiah 11:1)."[2]

2. In 5:7-9, summarize the influence that the remnant of God's people will have among the nations.

This remnant will triumph over Israel's enemies destroying them

3. In 5:10-15, what is the significance of what God promises to do?

The Lord will destroy everything that does not serve to worship him

Witchcraft . . . cast spells (5:12). "Seeking occult knowledge was explicitly forbidden in Israel (Deuteronomy 18:10,14)."[3]

4. Describe the "courtroom" scene being shown in Micah 6:1-5 and the "case" being made by the Lord.

the Lord is making a case against the people for not following him

126

asking how he has burdened them, relating all he has done for them, including bring them

out of Egypt

5. What is the correct answer to the questions the Lord asked the people in Micah 6:3?

the Lord didnot burden them rather he lead them to the promised land

For Further Study:
Review the questions asked in Micah 6:6-7. Explore the connections you see in the following verses:
1 Samuel 15:22; Psalm 51:16; Isaiah 1:11-15; Hosea 6:6.

Optional Application: What personal claim and calling upon your life do you see represented by the words of Micah 6:8?

6. a. Summarize in your own words the people's question in 6:6-7.

How are we supposed to come before the Lord, what does he want from me?

b. Explain the reply given in 6:8.

The Lord wants us to act justly to our neighbors, have mercy on others and not act like we are better than anyone else

___

Balak . . . Balaam (6:5). See Numbers 22–24.

___

7. What are the accusations made by the Lord in Micah 6:9-12, and who are these directed against?

all people in Jerusalem are guilty of cheating, violence, are liars,   *using false wights + measures*

127

Optional Application: How fully do the words of Micah 7:7 express your own heart attitude? What do these words mean personally in regard to your present and future?

they will not enjoy any of the fruits of their labor and what ever they have will be taken by the sword (war)

the Lord never fails your trust

8. What judgments does God pronounce in 6:13-16, and what is their significance?

He will destroy them, they will eat but not be satisfied their savings will amount to nothing, your heart will fail

9. What consequences of the people's disobedience are emphasized in Micah 7:1-6?

their will be no trust between people, not even between family members

10. a. What is most significant in Micah's convictions as expressed in 7:7?

belief in God and waiting for him as a Savior

b. What contrasts do you see between the message of 7:1-6 and the words of Micah in verse 7?

the only thing you can trust in the Lord all others are doubtful

11. How do the prophetic words of 7:8-10 emphasize repentance and faith?

Belief in the Lord will carry us through if we ask for help from him and confess our sins

Me . . . I . . . my (7:8-13). "The speakers are not identified but are probably personified cities."[4]

Rise (7:8). "In this military context," the word "signifies to rise from the state of defeat (Proverbs 24:16)."[5]

Because I have sinned against him, I will bear the LORD's wrath (7:9). "Lady Zion is ready to endure the fury of Yahweh for several reasons. First, she admits the punishment is deserved. . . . Second, the punishment is temporary ('until'). Third, the God of 'justice' will punish the malefactor and bring Zion out of humiliating captivity; it will then see his righteous salvation."[6]

12. Describe the future for God's people that is prophesied in 7:11-13.

> *Gods people will return to him from where ever they are*

People will come to you (7:12). "The prophecy finds fulfillment in the church, composed of all nations (Romans 4:16-17), which come to the heavenly Zion, the 'true' Zion, represented symbolically by the earthly city (Hebrews 12:22)."[7]

13. How do the words of 7:14-17 indicate a restored relationship between Israel and her God?

> *God provides for his people and if they follow him he will protect them and show them wonders and his power*

Optional Application: What truths in Micah 7:14-17 do you most want to praise and thank God for at this time?

14. What are the most significant truths about God that are brought to light in the closing words of this book (see 7:18-20)?

   God is a compassionate God
   who figures our transgressions

15. In Micah 5–7, what would you select as the key verse or passage—one that best captures or reflects the dynamics of what these chapters are all about?

   _5: 7 - 15_

16. What do these chapters in Micah communicate most to you about the heart and character of God?

   Failure to follow Gods
   word will lead to
   punishment

17. List any lingering questions you have about Micah 5–7.

Reviewing the book of Micah

18. What have you learned most or appreciated most in your study of the book of Micah?

_____

_____

_____

_____

19. Recall the message of Isaiah 55:10-11 — in the same way God sends rain and snow from the sky to water the earth and nurture life, so also He sends His words to accomplish specific purposes. What would you suggest are God's primary purposes for the message of Micah in the lives of His people today?

_____

_____

_____

_____

20. Review also the guidelines in Philippians 4:8 — "Whatever is true, whatever is noble, whatever is right, whatever is pure, whatever is lovely, whatever is admirable — if anything is excellent or praiseworthy — _think about such things_" (emphasis added). As you reflect on all you've read in this book of Micah, what stands out to you as being particularly _true_, or _noble_, or _right_, or _pure_, or _lovely_, or _admirable_, or _excellent_, or _praiseworthy_ — and therefore well worth thinking more about?

_____

_____

_____

_____

_____

Optional Application: Which verses in the book of Micah would be most helpful for you to memorize so you have them always available in your mind and heart for the Holy Spirit to use?

131

21. Considering that all of Scripture testifies ultimately of Christ, where does Jesus come most in focus for you in this book?

_____

_____

_____

_____

22. In your understanding, what are the strongest ways Micah points us to mankind's need for Jesus and for what He accomplished in His death and resurrection?

_____

_____

_____

_____

23. Recall Paul's reminder in Romans 15:4 that the Old Testament Scriptures can give us patience and perseverance as well as comfort and encouragement. In your own life, how do you see the book of Micah living up to Paul's description? In what ways do the Old Testament Scriptures help meet your personal need for both perseverance and encouragement?

_____

_____

_____

_____

For the group

Consider focusing your discussion for lesson 12 especially on some of the following issues, themes, and concepts recognized as major overall themes in Micah. Which of these are dealt with in some way in chapters 5–7, and how are they further developed there?

- God's judgment upon sin
- Salvation from God
- The sovereignty of God
- The future kingdom of God

Questions 15–23 in lesson 12 are among those that may stimulate your best and most helpful discussion.

Remember to look also at the "For Thought and Discussion" question in the margin.

1. *New Geneva Study Bible* (Nashville: Thomas Nelson, 1995), at Micah 5:2.
2. Bruce K. Waltke, "Micah," *The Minor Prophets*, ed. Thomas Edward McComiskey (Grand Rapids, MI: Baker, 2009), 703–704.
3. *ESV Study Bible* (Wheaton, IL: Crossway, 2008), at Micah 5:12-13.
4. *ESV*, at Micah 7:8-13.
5. Waltke, 754.
6. Waltke, 755.
7. Waltke, 756.

STUDY AIDS

For further information on the material in this study, consider the following sources. They are available on the Internet (www.christianbook.com, www.amazon.com, and so on), or your local Christian bookstore should be able to order any of them if it does not carry them. Most seminary libraries have them as well as many university and public libraries. If they are out of print, you might be able to find them online.

Commentaries on the Minor Prophets

Alexander, T. Desmond. *Jonah* (InterVarsity, 1988).

Allen, Leslie C. *The Books of Joel, Obadiah, Jonah, and Micah* (Eerdmans, 1976).

Andersen, Francis I. and David Noel Freedman. *Amos: A New Translation with Introduction and Commentary* (Doubleday, 1989).

Andersen, Francis I. and David Noel Freedman. *Hosea: A New Translation with Introduction and Commentary* (Doubleday, 1980).

Andersen, Francis I. and David Noel Freedman. *Micah: A New Translation with Introduction and Commentary* (Doubleday, 2000).

Baker, David W. *Obadiah* (InterVarsity, 1988).

Baldwin, Joyce. "Jonah," in *The Minor Prophets*, ed. Thomas Edward McComiskey (Baker, 2009).

Calvin, John. *Commentaries on the Twelve Minor Prophets*, 5 vols. (Eerdmans, 1950).

Crenshaw, James L. *Joel: New Translation with Introduction and Commentary* (Doubleday, 1995).

Dillard, Raymond Bryan. "Joel," in *Commentary on the Old Testament: The Minor Prophets*, ed. Thomas Edward McComiskey (Baker, 2009).

Fairbairn, Patrick. *Jonah: His Life, Character, and Mission* (Kregel, 1964).

Finley, Thomas J. *Joel, Amos, Obadiah* (Moody, 1990).

Hillers, Delbert R. *Micah: A Commentary on the Book of the Prophet Micah* (Fortress, 1984).

Keil, C. F. and F. Delitzsch. *Commentary on the Old Testament: The Minor Prophets*, vol. 10 (Hendrickson, 1996).

Kidner, Derek. *The Message of Hosea: Love to the Loveless* (InterVarsity, 1981).

Mays, James Luther. *Amos: A Commentary and Hosea: A Commentary* (Westminster, 1969).

Mays, James Luther. *Micah: A Commentary* (Westminster, 1976).

McComiskey, Thomas Edward. "Hosea," in *The Minor Prophets* (Baker, 2009).

Motyer, J. A. *The Message of Amos: The Day of the Lion* (InterVarsity, 1974).

Niehaus, Jeff. "Amos," and "Obadiah," in *The Minor Prophets*, ed. Thomas Edward McComiskey (Baker, 2009).

Paul, Shalom M. *Amos: A Commentary on the Book of Amos* (Fortress, 1991).

Raabe, Paul R. *Obadiah: A New Translation with Introduction and Commentary* (Doubleday, 1996).

Smith, Gary V. *Amos: A Commentary* (Regency, 1989).

Stuart, Douglas. *Hosea–Jonah* (Word Books, 1987).

Waltke, Bruce K. "Micah," in *The Minor Prophets*, ed. Thomas Edward McComiskey (Baker, 2009).

Wolff, Hans Walter. *Hosea: A Commentary on the Book of the Prophet Hosea* (Fortress, 1974).

Wolff, Hans Walter. *Micah: A Commentary* (Augsburg, 1990).

Wolff, Hans Walter. *Obadiah and Jonah: A Commentary* (Augsburg, 1986).

Historical background sources and handbooks

Bible study becomes more meaningful when modern Western readers understand the times and places in which the biblical authors lived. *The IVP Bible Background Commentary: Old Testament*, by John H. Walton, Victor H. Matthews, and Mark Chavalas (InterVarsity, 2000), provides insight into the ancient Near Eastern world, its peoples, customs, and geography to help contemporary readers better understand the context in which the Old Testament Scriptures were written.

A **handbook** of biblical customs can also be useful. Some good ones are the time-proven updated classic *Halley's Bible Handbook with the New International Version*, by Henry H. Halley (Zondervan, 2007), and the inexpensive paperback *Manners and Customs in the Bible*, by Victor H. Matthews (Hendrickson, 1991).

Concordances, dictionaries, and encyclopedias

A **concordance** lists words of the Bible alphabetically along with each verse in which the word appears. It lets you do your own word studies. An *exhaustive* concordance lists every word used in a given translation, while an *abridged* or *complete* concordance omits either some words, some occurrences of the word, or both.

Two of the best exhaustive concordances are *Strong's Exhaustive Concordance* and *The Strongest NIV Exhaustive Concordance*. *Strong's* is available based on the KJV and NASB. *Strong's* has an index by which you can find out which Greek or Hebrew word is used in a given English verse. The NIV concordance does the same thing except it also includes an index for Aramaic words in the original texts from which the NIV was translated. However, neither concordance requires knowledge of the original languages. *Strong's* is available online at www.biblestudytools.com. Both are also available in hard copy.

A **Bible dictionary** or **Bible encyclopedia** alphabetically lists articles about people, places, doctrines, important words, customs, and geography of the Bible.

Holman Illustrated Bible Dictionary, edited by C. Brand, C. W. Draper, and A. England (B&H, 2003), offers more than seven hundred color photos, illustrations, and charts; sixty full-color maps; and up-to-date archeological findings, along with exhaustive definitions of people, places, things, and events—dealing with every subject in the Bible. It uses a variety of Bible translations and is the only dictionary that includes the HCSB, NIV, KJV, RSV, NRSV, REB, NASB, ESV, and TEV.

The New Unger's Bible Dictionary, Revised and Expanded, by Merrill F. Unger (Moody, 2006), has been a bestseller for more than fifty years. Its 6,700-plus entries reflect the most current scholarship and more than 1,200,000 words are supplemented with detailed essays, colorful photography and maps, and dozens of charts and illustrations to enhance your understanding of God's Word. Based on the NASB.

The Zondervan Encyclopedia of the Bible, edited by Moisés Silva and Merrill C. Tenney (Zondervan, 2008), is excellent and exhaustive. However, its five 1,000-page volumes are a financial investment, so all but very serious students may prefer to use it at a church, public, college, or seminary library.

Unlike a Bible dictionary in the above sense, *Vine's Complete Expository Dictionary of Old and New Testament Words*, by W. E. Vine, Merrill F. Unger, and William White Jr. (Thomas Nelson, 1996), alphabetically lists major words used in the KJV and defines each Old Testament Hebrew or New Testament Greek word the KJV translates with that English word. *Vine's* lists verse references where that Hebrew or Greek word appears so that you can do your own cross-references and word studies without knowing the original languages.

The Brown-Driver-Briggs Hebrew and English Lexicon by Francis Brown, C. Briggs, and S. R. Driver (Hendrickson, 1996), is probably the most respected and comprehensive Bible lexicon for Old Testament studies. *BDB* gives not only dictionary definitions for each word but relates each word to its Old Testament usage and categorizes its nuances of meaning.

Bible atlases and map books

A **Bible atlas** can be a great aid to understanding what is going on in a book of the Bible and how geography affected events. Here are a few good choices:

The Hammond Atlas of Bible Lands (Langenscheidt, 2007) packs a ton of resources into just sixty-four pages. It contains maps, of course, but also photographs, illustrations, and a comprehensive timeline. It includes an introduction to the unique geography of the Holy Land, including terrain, trade routes, vegetation, and climate information.

The New Moody Atlas of the Bible, by Barry J. Beitzel (Moody, 2009), is scholarly, very evangelical, and full of theological text, indexes, and references. Beitzel shows vividly how God prepared the land of Israel perfectly for the acts of salvation He was going to accomplish in it.

Then and Now Bible Maps Insert (Rose, 2008) is a nifty paperback that is sized just right to fit inside your Bible cover. Only forty-four pages long, it features clear plastic overlays of modern-day cities and countries so you can see what nation or city now occupies the Bible setting you are reading about. Every major city of the Bible is included.

For small-group leaders

Discipleship Journal's Best Small-Group Ideas, Vols. 1 and 2 (NavPress, 2005). Each volume is packed with 101 of the best hands-on tips and group-building principles from *Discipleship Journal's* "Small Group Letter" and "DJ Plus" as well as articles from the magazine. They will help you inject new passion into the life of your small group.

Donahue, Bill. *Leading Life-Changing Small Groups* (Zondervan, 2002). This comprehensive resource is packed with information, practical tips, and insights that will teach you about small-group philosophy and structure, discipleship, conducting meetings, and more.

McBride, Neal F. *How to Build a Small-Groups Ministry* (NavPress, 1994). *How to Build a Small-Groups Ministry* is a time-proven, hands-on workbook for pastors and lay leaders that includes everything you need to know to develop a plan that fits your unique church. Through basic principles, case studies, and worksheets, McBride leads you through twelve logical steps for organizing and administering a small-groups ministry.

McBride, Neal F. *How to Lead Small Groups* (NavPress, 1990). This book covers leadership skills for all kinds of small groups: Bible study, fellowship, task, and support groups. It's filled with step-by-step guidance and practical exercises to help you grasp the critical aspects of small-group leadership and dynamics.

Miller, Tara, and Jenn Peppers. *Finding the Flow: A Guide for Leading Small Groups and Gatherings* (IVP Connect, 2008). *Finding the Flow* offers a fresh take on leading small groups by seeking to develop the leader's small-group facilitation skills.

Bible study methods

Discipleship Journal's Best Bible Study Methods (NavPress, 2002). This is a collection of thirty-two creative ways to explore Scripture that will help you enjoy studying God's Word more.

Hendricks, Howard, and William Hendricks. *Living by the Book: The Art and Science of Reading the Bible* (Moody, 2007). *Living by the Book* offers a practical three-step process that will help you master simple yet effective inductive methods of observation, interpretation, and application that will make all the difference in your time with God's Word. A workbook by the same title is also available to go along with the book.

The Navigator Bible Studies Handbook (NavPress, 1994). This resource teaches the underlying principles for doing good inductive Bible study, including instructions on doing question-and-answer studies, verse-analysis studies, chapter-analysis studies, and topical studies.

Warren, Rick. *Rick Warren's Bible Study Methods: Twelve Ways You Can Unlock God's Word* (HarperCollins, 2006). Rick Warren offers simple, step-by-step instructions, guiding you through twelve different approaches to studying the Bible for yourself with the goal of becoming more like Jesus.

Encounter God's Word
Experience LifeChange

LifeChange by The Navigators

The LifeChange Bible study series can help you grow in Christ-likeness through a life-changing encounter with God's Word. Discover what the Bible says, and develop the skills and desire to dig even deeper into God's Word. Each study includes study aids and discussion questions.

NAVESSENTIALS

Voices of The Navigators—Past, Present, and Future

NAVESSENTIALS offer core Navigator messages from such authors as Jim Downing, LeRoy Eims, Mike Treneer, and more — at an affordable price. This new series will deeply influence generations in the movement of discipleship. Learn from the old and new messages of The Navigators how powerful and transformational the life of a disciple truly is.

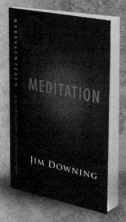
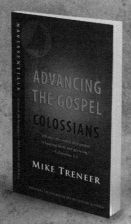
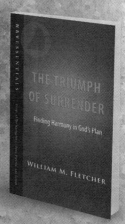

Meditation
by Jim Downing
9781615217250 | $5.00

Advancing the Gospel
by Mike Treneer
9781617471575 | $5.00

The Triumph of Surrender
by William M. Fletcher
9781615219070 | $5.00

Available wherever books are sold.   NAVPRESS